Furniture Care and Conservation

FURNITURE CARE
and CONSERVATION

Revised, Third Edition

ROBERT F. McGIFFIN

Foreword by Caroline K. Keck

AASLH Press
American Association for
State and Local History
Nashville, Tennessee

Every attempt has been made to provide the reader of this volume with current information. The author and AASLH endorse no particular products or methods. Nor do they assume responsibility for adverse health effects or artifact degradation resulting from the use of any procedures presented.

Library of Congress Cataloguing-in-Publication Data

McGiffin, Robert F., 1942-
    Furniture care and conservation.

    Bibliography: p.
    Includes index.
    1. Furniture—Repairing. I. Title.
TT199.M4   1989   749' .1'0288   89-6610
ISBN 0-942063-22-8

First Printing 1983
Second Edition, Revised 1989
Third Edition, Revised 1992

To Barbara and Kimberly

Contents

Foreword

Except for those who advise the lovelorn, most people who give advice are unlikely to win popularity contests. This is especially true if the proffered advice is for one's own good. When others emphasize what you should do and how you should go about it, flatly stating what you should *not* do and why you should not do it, the information is palatable only when it is clearly objective.

In giving advice throughout this book, Robert McGiffin is objective. He quite obviously cares about the preservation of furniture. His book of practical instructions is intended to enable a reader sharing the same concern to provide the best possible tender, loving care any amateur could offer a collection of furniture.

I use the term *amateur* in its literal meanings. Mr. Webster tells us an amateur is someone who performs for the pleasure of it, rather than for money, and he implies also that such a person has a relative lack of skill. There are many levels of skill; and like other forms of competence, these skills diminish only when their possessors attempt to exceed their appropriate level. When the additional venture assumes a higher, deeper, wider scope of activities than one's competence may encompass, the usual result is disaster.

The relationship between a serious amateur and a serious professional is seldom antagonistic. Neither wants to ask too much of the other. However, those on the perimeter who are neither the one nor the other often magnify evidences of performances and voice complaints on what they view as unwarranted differentiations. There are differentiations in skill, in knowledge, and in experience that make it a safety factor rather than a pretension to superiority for a professional to limit the extent of his or her published advice. No conservator, including me, views our special expertise as a secret skill, but none of us wishes to detail instructions that cannot readily be followed and that might result in damages to an artifact. There are no instant experts, and the voices of experience appropriately limit advices.

In the field of artifact conservation, mistakes range from the sad-but-harmless to the unrealized-but-inevitably-fatal. Many mistakes relate to unforeseen, unanticipated reactions, reactions that are predictable on the part of the artifact under given circumstances. Discovering what some of these reactions can be will doubtless come to many a reader like the confirmation of a nagging worry. So much of what McGiffin repeats and repeats, hammering home its importance, is bound to have passed through the minds of his readers. Subconsciously, almost all personnel active in historic houses have at one time or another sensed the problems in preserving historical integrity, sensed the weight of decision involved in collection maintenance, factors of ethical evaluation that McGiffin so neatly articulates. The prime concentration, he insists, is on the *object:* do not compromise its integrity; do not remove anything that shows the way it was used; do not let replacement of missing parts disfigure the object and distort the intent of the original maker. All these prohibitions clarify and vocalize what sensitive caretakers have felt for years. A great merit of this book is in its intimacy to the thoughts of its readers.

In discussing the principles that guide contemporary conservation treatment, *reversibility* is stressed: try not to do anything in the course of a remedial treatment that cannot be *undone* in the future without exposing the artifact to harm. Sound and very wise, when you think it out. Those of us in the older generation know from bitter experience how crucial it is for the survival of the object never to consider our own labors as a final solution. Everything ages: materials in repairs as well as materials in the original, and almost everything will have to be done over before the century is out. When substances used for repair are tougher than the parts they rejoin, first, they are likely to place undue strain on the surrounding, weaker matter; and second, attempts to remove such materials will physically disrupt if not destroy adjacent portions of the original. There are exceptions to that rule, and McGiffin mentions some.

It may also be remarked that certain operations where reversibility is seldom weighed are, in themselves, irreversible. Take cleaning, for instance: how do you put back what you took away, except by attempts to *replace* it? A cleaning can go too far, can take away what it should have left in place, can break the surface of an ancient finish. Not consciously visualized as moments of irreversibility, cleaning activities nevertheless are such. All McGiffin's warnings on testing cleaning mixtures and proceeding with caution are very much to the point.

Evidence of an object's functional use can so easily be removed, accidentally and without intent. I am reminded of a story a colleague told on himself. He was an expert practitioner in conservation of paper artifacts. Our government sent him several newly discovered and sorely abused checks, signed by no less than President Abraham Lincoln. My friend spent hours of patient attention operating on the damages to restore the checks to their entire whole. To his distress, when he returned the checks, he learned that he had obliterated their cancellations, at that period accomplished by pressing a check down and over a sharp triangular cutting stand. That fact might have been within the knowledge of a specialist in historical banking techniques, but it definitely was not general knowledge nor the normal concept of cancellation marks. I feel that the fault was with the curator who failed to warn the conservator that one set of cuts was evidence of functional use. This misfortune occurred more than twenty-five years ago, and it is conceivable that a similarly expert paper conservator practicing today might have requested and received precise data on the implications of all damages recorded in his preliminary report. That precaution might have eliminated the improper repairs of the triangular slashes and preserved the cancelled status of Mr. Lincoln's checks.

Formal training in the practice of artifact conservation has made an appreciable difference in expectation of performance. I am well aware that no matter how extensive and how excellent the offered training may be, not everyone who gains it is equally competent, or ethical, or dedicated. That can apply to doctors and lawyers and teachers as much as to conservators. What formal training does offer to those who receive it is the opportunity for background knowledge in a range and depth of academic benefits. That type of exposure is not readily available to craftsmen. Uniformity in the basic training of conservators renders thorough examination prior to treatment a matter of routine, just as it makes certain categories of testing and investigation routine. The willingness to perform routines, as well as the quality of such performance, admittedly cannot be guaranteed. Recognition of the advantages these services afford toward the optimum kind of treatment, the best selection of treatment for the object at hand, is an attribute derived from academic instructions in the practice of conservation.

I never attended an academic training program in conservation. I met my husband, Sheldon Keck, in 1931 at the Fogg Art Museum in the first "course" either of us ever took relating to conservation. It was a very generalized instruction, stimulating, but not exacting. My professional education has come mostly from my husband, a natural expert in the field; from my colleagues, who shared acquired knowledge as they acquired it; and from long—and not unoccasionally mortifying—experience in working. During the early years of our museum positions, my husband and I took apprentices. Even in the beginning we sought to provide a broader understanding of the field than could be supplied by treatments at hand. Apprenticeships were never satisfactory to us; we found ourselves endeavoring to formalize elementary requisites for professional development. Under the auspices of New York University, we attempted teaching the principles of art conservation at the laboratory of the Brooklyn Museum; but one day a week—even for fifteen weeks—was hardly sufficient education, and Keck efforts turned toward the initiation of academic instruction in the professional practice of art conservation in the United States.

Eventually, as McGiffin's appendix lists indicate, various examples of such graduate training came to be. Post facto, I am convinced that we went about it the wrong way: we should have tried planting a beginning at the undergraduate level, so that any postgraduate specialization might be a natural instead of an alien development, as natural a procedure as a Ph.D. in art history. I firmly believe that if our labor is to be accredited with the respect and attention it merits, every student who yearns for knowledge in some aspect of artifact study should have background instruction in the way that particular category of artifact was fabricated down through history, what the behavior of the materials were that formed it, and what means may be employed for the physical examination of extant examples, their condition, their possible authenticity, possible alterations and possible original remains. A common appreciation of these elementary facts would provide our society with a group of amateurs and professionals who understand one another's concerns. Perhaps this will come to pass. Here and there, colleges across the country are showing an interest in offering such teachings to their students in applied art and art history. The result could be a community bonanza for preservation.

I would never deny that there are craftsmen as skilled as academically trained conservators—some of them even more so. Usually, however, craftsmen lack what I call "the view from the hill": a perspective over-view of an entire assembly of related problems in care. Perhaps many of the problems McGiffin cites in this book, irritating problems, appear peripheral to the preservation of furniture; but after reading what he has to say about light levels, relative humidity, fumigation, shipping—even simple handling—of artifacts, the reader will agree that none of those considerations may safely be ignored. Each, in its own nasty little way, can make or break survival chances for a piece of furniture. In my opinion, the average craftsman, regardless of the skill he may have attained, has never been exposed to the intensified atmosphere of care that instructs an academically trained practitioner, and so cannot be expected to share the same onus of responsibility for the whole that one may expect of the professional.

That is a generalization on my part; take it as you wish. I have known fine craftsmen, deeply concerned with the externals of preservation as well as with the quality of their remedial treatments. The inclusion in this book's appendix of the Code of Ethics drafted by our professional organization will explain, better than I can, the necessary disciplines. Certainly it will demonstrate standards of procedure that an employer may anticipate will be followed by those who have been academically trained.

With no intention of playing devil's advocate, I would remind the thoughtful reader that the concept of an inviolate integrity for artifacts fabricated by man is of recent origin and is by no means unanimous, even in the twentieth century. In centuries past, created works, whether among the fine or the functional arts, were constantly altered to suit changes in tastes and needs. Restoration was the activity employed to disguise damages to an object and/or to modernize it. Alterations in size, color, and shape were normal occurrences and distressed few owners. Painted portraits were trimmed to fit wall spaces; manuscripts were rubbed clean to be reused for immediate texts; an abraded polychrome statue might easily be gilded over to meet the whim of an owner. Nobody objected, so long as the work satisfied the client; and if it didn't, why worry?—it could always be done over again. An odd status quo de-veloped in the nineteenth century with the strengthening preference for accepting symbols of age (layers of obscurity, "Golden Glow" or "Museum Soup" coverings) as the stamp of antiquity. Cleaning was an abomination—a veil of dirt, a desideratum. None of this was very long ago. The twentieth century attitude that all that's hidden is not necessarily old, and the more modern preference for factual investigation are still not universally accepted.

Irrespective of current controversies over who cleans *what* when, and how—which confuse the public and distract attention from serious preservation problems—there is a mounting sympathy for sound principles of collection care. Meaningful efforts must include *complete* physical examination and sensitive evaluation of historical and aesthetic significance. Greater attention is being paid to systems for accurate recording, testing, weighing of findings, and planned treatment proposals. Procedures tend to become increasingly cautious. As McGiffin points out, this is all to the good. The fabrications of man and the preservation problems presented by each man-made thing will continue to be unique. The public has come to realize that there are no panaceas, any more than there are instant experts to execute them if they did exist.

The message of this book parallels my own message as a conservator of paintings. The first priority, if the least glamorous function of a conservator, is to provide protective maintenance for the artifacts in one's care. The second is to stabilize (where feasible) the original remains. Sometimes the rejoining of separated parts is enough to ensure survival; sometimes it is insufficient, because it fails to unify an image. Restoration, that minimal addition to missing portions to achieve the satisfaction of the naked eye, is a third priority. Particularly in painting conservation, this is the part of our work that causes the most disagreement. And quite naturally so, for what satisfies the eye of one individual does not satisfy every eye, and never will. However, whether in painting conservation or furniture conservation, if *the first two priorities* have been performed to the best of our ability, the artifact can outlive changing whims in its cosmetic make-up. The body beneath the so-appropriately-reversible surface alterations will survive.

Madame Gilberte Emile-Mâle, who is in charge of conservation in the National Museums of France, likened our patrimony—the cultural estate we have inherited from our forefathers—to Ariadne's thread. She reminds us that this thread, stretching between the past and the future to permit a feeling of continuity across centuries, is fragile and must not be broken. Such a lovely simile for conservators and for all of us willing to accept responsibility for care. I do believe that acceptance of this responsibility for the care of furniture will be finely enhanced for everyone benefiting from the guidance of this book.

CAROLINE K. KECK
Cooperstown, New York
1982

ACKNOWLEDGMENTS

I owe a great deal to the people who aided me in completing this book.

Rostislav Hlopoff has been a considerable help since I began my career and during the writing of this book. He has always been unselfish and willing to help me and any other students of his, day or night.

Thanks to William Tyrrell for his voluntary editing of the early manuscript.

Additional people who gave me help, advice, and encouragement include Caroline and Sheldon Keck, F. Christopher Tahk, Dan Kushel, Joyce Zucker, Gary Gore, Ron DuCharme, Richard Sherin, Heidi Miksch, Kathy Cunningham, Kristin Gibbons, Bill Stevenson, Joan Cash, Betty Elder, and Martha Strayhorn, and many others.

I am also indebted to Colonel Edward Gilbert and Carl Wesenberg, who supervised my internship during 1975 and 1976 at the Greenfield Village and Henry Ford Museum Conservation Center.

Additional thanks to James Gold for permission to publish the photographs of the New York State Collections.

And special thanks to my wife Barbara, who spent much of the winter of 1980–1981 typing and retyping all of the rough and final drafts of the manuscript for this book. Thanks also—and apologies—to our daughter Kimberly, for the time and attention taken from her while this work was in progress.

Furniture Care and Conservation

❧ 1 ❧
Introduction:
Restoration and Conservation

THERE are distinct differences in the way one approaches the safekeeping and protective treatment of functional artifacts and historical objects, such as old furniture. In American terminology, one approach to the care of such artifacts is broadly entitled *restoration;* another is called *conservation.*

Restoration can be defined as the practice of repairing or reconstructing an object to return it to its original condition and/or appearance.

Conservation can be defined as the practice of protecting an object from injury, loss, or violation.

One who practices restoration (a restorer) of old furniture may advocate removing from a venerable piece of furniture a finish that has deteriorated with age, while a person who practices conservation (a conservator) may advocate retaining the finish and trying to stabilize it to prevent further deterioration.

Often, the best of these two approaches to furniture care merge, and some of the ideas and procedures used in the two approaches overlap. Both conservators and restorers would agree, for example, with the idea of replacing an integral part that is missing from a piece of furniture— say, a chair leg, which is necessary not only to stabilize the object, but also to complete the original basic design.

Frequently, both restorer and conservator are well versed in techniques for examining, cleaning, moving, storing, and protecting old furniture and artifacts; and in most countries, the terms *conservator* and *restorer* are synonymous, though they are not now considered so in the United States. One difference between the two schools of thought is that

Fig. 1.1. The fragment of ribbon still visible here on the post of a child's cradle was probably attached long ago for decoration, when the cradle was in active use. Because of what such things tell us about the people who put them there, items like the ribbon should be kept intact as important parts of the total historical representation.

the conservator's training, experience, and knowledge are focused on trying to save darkened, scratched, cracked, unsteady pieces of furniture from further spoilation—while preserving the historical integrity evidenced in the scars of usage left on each piece—Oliver Cromwell's "warts and all" approach. The restorer's trained eye sees the beauty of a battered piece as it must once have been, pristine new, and hard-worn restorers' skills and techniques are bent toward stripping away the dull, marred finish, sanding and scraping off cracks and scratches, cleaning each part until it seems shiny new—to present the restored object looking as if it were freshly made.

In past years, numerous publications have appeared, explaining ways of restoring and repairing furniture; but only a handful in recent years provide information on the philosophy of furniture conservation. That is why this book has been written: to present an alternative approach to the treatment of historic furniture and wooden artifacts.

Only recently has conservation begun to gain recognition as an emerging profession. The National Conservation Advisory Council, now known as the National Institute for the Conservation of Cultural Property, reports that only within the last five or six decades have truly well-designed conservation education programs become available in the United States. [1]

Initially, emphasis in conservation programs was on the examination and treatment of paintings only. Gradually, attention was also focused on objects composed mainly of paper. Starting about 1972, there has been a growing emphasis on conservation of three-dimensional objects, including furniture. Even as late as 1978, however, there were, in the entire United States, possibly only ten furniture conservators[2] whose standards of practice were in accordance with the Murray Pease code of ethics,[3] a code first drawn up in 1967 by the International Institute for Conservation of Historic and Artistic Works–American Group (IIC-AG) Committee on Professional Standards, under the direction of Murray Pease, Conservator, Metropolitan Museum of Art. This American group is now called the American Institute for Conservation of Historic and Artistic Works (AIC), and its official Code of Ethics and Standards of Practice (the Murray Pease code), expanded in 1979, appears in full as Appendix 1 of this book.

Scholars have long been aware that each artifact is unique. When an artifact, or any part of it, is destroyed, a part of history is lost and can

Fig. 1.2. The wide split in this wooden clock face points up the constant need for careful planning in conservation practices. The break occurred when the batten visible beneath the clock face was attached to the back of it, in an attempt to hold the curve of the dial rigid. The resultant stress caused the thin wood of the dial to crack.

never be recovered. An increasing general awareness of that fact may help to change significantly many of the methods of caring for, interpreting, and protecting historic and artistic works.

Furniture, created for utilitarian purposes in a living environment, predictably undergoes strains, dents, burns, and assorted abrasions, and each such occurrence is a record of the object's use. The eighteenth-century infant who pounds his spoon on a tabletop and the mother who, trying to keep warm, moves her chair too close to the fireplace are adding to the surface of that furniture an interpretable record of its use. I believe that sanding or scraping away such dents and burns destroys forever an important part of any wooden artifact; and from a baldly economic point of view, a zealous finisher intent on removing clear physical evidence of a family's usage is also reducing the monetary value of the object, as well as destroying palpable history. Informed collectors will avoid any object that has suffered such restoration abuse.

Fig. 1.3. Conservators working to repair a split across the face of an old wooden clock (see fig. 1.2) found that a modern-day nail, driven into the wood to attach a brace behind the dial, had forced one side of the dial's curve flat, causing the rest of the wood to warp and split. The nail also caused irreparable damage in penetrating layers of paint and going through the wooden dial support.

Those who own or are responsible for a historical object must also hold its care paramount. Kept in good condition, even simple household objects may one day be, for some museum collection, visible representations of long-vanished aspects of a way of living. Each year, the number of Americans who recognize either the names or the usage of such once-common articles as washboards and pie-safes grows fewer. Authentic evidence of the historical reality of former centuries will not be available to future generations if household objects are uniformly restored to twentieth-century condition.

This book is not written as a treatise for conservators, and it will not make conservators of its readers. However, it *will* provide recommendations for the private collector, the hard-working staff of the small historical society, the museum professional, and all others truly concerned about the care and preservation of furniture.

1.4

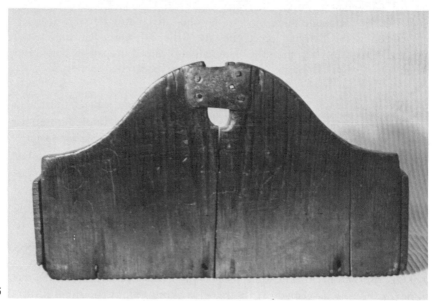

1.5

1.6

Figs. 1.4, 1.5, and *1.6.* A long-ago do-it-yourselfer shaped and nailed on a small iron plate to mend a break in this salt box. The true conservator considering the whole object today would leave such patchwork intact, as part of the whole object's history. Nothing would be gained, now, by removing the plate and replacing the lost wood it took the place of; besides, it tells us something about human ingenuity during the period it represents. So far as physical preservation of the object itself is concerned, the wood reached an equilibrium with the fasteners long ago; although minor checks developed (see fig. 1.6), they are essentially stable.

Fig. 1.7. Detail of an early sofa stretcher. Not only did a recent reupholstering detract from the original design; it also caused irreparable damage during its attachment. Because the original bamboo turning would not allow for a smooth edge, it was removed with a rasp.

Fig. 1.8. The surface of the jelly cupboard shown here is covered with dents, scratches, and traces of early paint. The door still swings on hinges old enough to be the original ones. All such bits of historical evidence should be preserved: to try to restore this piece of furniture to a like-new condition by sanding the surface and polishing the hinges would be both misguided and destructive.

～～ 2 ～～
Environment and Its Effects
on Wooden Artifacts

O NE of the first considerations that must be taken into account in providing proper care for any furniture collection is the environment in which the collection will be kept.

Environment can have devastating effects on furniture—more so, perhaps, than on any other type of artifact. This is due primarily to the materials of which furniture is usually made—a variety of permeable, ultimately perishable materials, most of them wood and other organic substances, each reacting with the environment in a different way.

Wood expands and contracts as the moisture content of the surrounding air changes. This expansion-contraction characteristic of wood has long fueled the misconception about "breathing wood" that is brought back into understanding by Bruce Hoadley's article "Wood Has To Breathe, Doesn't It?".[1] Organic materials absorb moisture as the humidity in the air increases; they release moisture as the humidity level drops lower. These fluctuations in moisture content result in accelerating decomposition.

Environmental factors can also nullify conservation or restoration repair work. Regardless of how well repairs to furniture are executed, environmental elements that are not controlled can take a fearful toll. That is especially true of work with wood inlays, veneer, and finish work, and to a lesser extent with fills, inserts, and joint work.

I have seen this sort of thing happen countless times: the conservator completes repair work on a piece of furniture. Returned to its permanent place—where there are few or no environmental controls—the piece once more develops the identical problems for which the conservator repaired it.

12

Fig. 2.1. Fluctuations in humidity cause wooden structures to expand and contract repeatedly. Such humidity variations were a basic cause of the cracks marring the surface of this cabinet. The wood of the basic box over which the veneer was applied—the secondary structure—expanded and contracted at a rate different from that of the veneer overlay, resulting in the cracking of the thinner wood.

Humidity and Temperature

Ideally, furniture should be stored in a stable environment, where both humidity and temperature can be rigidly controlled. The atmosphere where wooden artifacts are housed should properly be controlled to

Fig. 2.2. The entire structure of this pianoforte warped out of plane when the instrument was placed directly over a heat duct.

a 50 percent relative humidity, plus or minus 5 percent, and a temperature of 68 degrees Fahrenheit, plus or minus 5 degrees.

Relative humidity is determined by comparing the amount of moisture present in the air of a given environment to the maximum amount of moisture the air could hold at the same temperature. Relative humidity expressed as a percentage indicates the amount of moisture in the air at a given time and temperature. Further information on relative humidity appears in Technical Bulletins 1, 3, and 5 of the Canadian Conservation Institute.

Museums being constructed today usually are built with controls to keep their environments within the ideal ranges of 50 percent relative humidity and 68 degrees Fahrenheit. It is alarmingly easy, however, to abuse even these sophisticated environmental systems. A curator at one such institution that I visited mentioned that much of the collection housed there was falling apart. A bit of detective work revealed that a thrifty administrator felt that the environmental controls had been installed there only for the comfort of the institution's visitors—and the system had been ordered shut down every night and restarted before visiting hours the next morning, which created constant fluctuations in the humidity. (One rationale for that action was that the artifacts in the collection had survived just fine, anyway, for two hundred years or more, without environmental controls!)

The first step toward controlling humidity and temperature in buildings that house wooden artifacts is to monitor the environment and find the trouble spots; then, correct whatever problems are found.

Humidity above about 70 percent is high, and furniture housed in such an environment can develop swelling of materials; softening of adhesives; cleavage of inlay, veneer, paint, or lacquer; mold growth; corrosion of metallic elements; and blooming on finishes.

Furniture housed in an environment where the humidity is too *low*—below about 30 percent—can develop shrinkage of materials; embrittlement of adhesives; cleavage or cracking of inlay, veneer, paint, or lacquer; structural-joint separations; loosening of screws, nails, pegs, and pins; and drying out of finishes.

Humidity control and measurement. Many types of equipment for

Fig. 2.3. Warped tabletops are a common problem. Attempts to hold them flat are rarely successful, however, and often result in further damage in the form of checks or splits in the wood of the top. The best solution is a stable environment.

monitoring relative humidity are available. Some are inexpensive and, while their accuracy is questionable, they can at least point out where problems exist. Any inexpensive thermometer indicates temperature levels.

Enough humidification and dehumidification units can be bought to keep the environment where a collection is housed within desirable limits. Above all, *it is vitally important to maintain a stable level of both temperature and humidity.* Control units must be tended and maintained daily. If they are forgotten for a single day, humidity can change drastically within only a few hours, causing traumatic shock to vulnerable artifacts. I have seen this happen: at a New York state site, one humidifier, running in an especially dry room, was forgotten for a few days, and the moisture level in the room rapidly dropped. The result: large splits along the grain in a wooden cup and two other valuable objects.

Two devices that measure humidity are a *psychrometer* and a *hygrometer.* The psychrometer measures only dry-bulb and wet-bulb temperatures; the hygrometer measures the relative humidity. A hygrometer

Fig. 2.4. Some of the finish on the back of this painted chest has flaked off. The cause: exposure to dampness.

that provides a graphic record is called a *hygrograph*. A hygrograph that also records temperature is called a *thermohygrograph*.

A thermohygrograph must be calibrated, and a small amount of basic information is needed to operate one properly. Also, a psychrometer is needed for calibration. Budgeting for one—or several—thermohygrographs should receive the highest priority from any institution that can afford them. Without such devices, discussions with consultants will not be meaningful, and environmental problems won't be specific.

All of the instruments mentioned here are available from laboratory supply houses, many of which are listed in Appendix 6. Additional information about such instruments can be found in the bulletins of the Canadian Conservation Institute.

If, after measuring the humidity in your building, you find it too high—above 70 percent—install a dehumidifier. You may need several dehumidifiers, depending on the volume of space you wish to control. If you have a good many dehumidifiers, one continuing chore will be just keeping them emptied of water. That chore can be simplified by having them connected to the building's plumbing system, so that the water empties off down the drain.

If your humidity measurement reading indicates that the environment is too dry—below 30 percent—install one or more humidifiers.

As a supplement to your humidifier, or in border-line environments, a full teakettle placed on top of a wood-burning stove, or a pan of water set on a heat register, can help increase the humidity. Even a sponge in a saucer kept full of water and placed under a piece of furniture will help a little bit—though only in small zones; and the saucer will have to be refilled frequently.

Temperature control. If you are one of the many who work or live in an older building, it is easy to say that all you have to do to protect your collection and the building is simply to control the interior environment, and all will be well. The nationwide energy conservation program, in emphasizing temperature control, has encouraged that viewpoint. However, recent experience has shown us that, while installing new insulation may reduce the fuel bill, that procedure may be the worst possible thing to do for a historic structure or a museum housing wooden artifacts.

Whenever you are considering major building modifications, such as installing new insulation in a historic structure, I should recommend first

Fig. 2.5. The wood in the two chests shown here will soon be damaged if the chests are kept as close to the heat duct as they are in the photograph—too close.

getting in touch with an old-house expert or an architect experienced in working with old buildings. One useful source of information for dealing with these and other problems is the *Old House Journal,* published in Brooklyn. The full address is in the bibliography. Insulating simply on the advice of a salesperson could be inviting major structural problems.

If you do have insulation installed, fiberglass insulation batts with a vapor barrier should be used for walls. Blown or foamed-in-place insulation without vapor barriers can result in peeling paint: without a vapor barrier, when water vapor migrates from inside the house and comes in contact with the cold insulation, it condenses; the resulting moisture makes the insulation soggy, and that eventually leads to dry rot, especially in the sills.

Attic spaces should be given high priority in installing insulation, because more than 20 percent of a building's heat is lost through the roof. Install attic insulation batts with the vapor barrier next to the ceiling of the room below. Do not insulate under upstairs rooms and attic floor boards if there isn't enough room for air to circulate to prevent rot.

During the summer, attic fans are excellent to reduce heat build-up. Reproductions of slow-running two- or four-bladed late nineteenth- and early twentieth-century ceiling fans are now available for circulating hot air away from ceilings in the summer and during the heating season. A small circulating fan can be helpful, also, in reducing the possibility of mold formation in damp areas. With the furniture itself, open drawers and cabinet doors of case pieces routinely to allow for air circulation throughout.

During winter weather, drafts of cold air circulating through a building that houses wooden artifacts should be eliminated—not only to conserve energy, but also to protect objects in the collection. Avoid placing furniture next to a doorway or a drafty window, where cold wind can blow in. Seal all cracks around windows and doors with weatherstripping or caulking.

In cold weather, thermal drapes help to retain warm air when the heat is on. Energy conservationists recommend that drapes be kept open during daylight hours, to admit warming sunlight. Owners of artifact collections must weigh that advice, however, against the knowledge that strong light of all kinds can hasten deterioration of some artifacts in all collections.

Light and the Nearby Artifact

All types of light cause cumulative damage to organic materials, and it should be remembered that a *low* light level over a long period of time can cause as much damage as a *high* light level for a short time.

Direct sunlight contains ultraviolet and infrared light levels that cause deterioration in materials used in furniture construction, especially furniture finishes. Several photographs in this book graphically document the effects of sunlight on finishes—see figures 2.6 and 12.8.

An easy way to keep out sunlight is to close drapes or pull down window shades during sunny periods of the day. Awnings and shutters are other devices to keep out sunlight. In institutions housing artifacts, the staff can set up a time schedule for maintenance people to follow for darkening rooms.

Like sunlight, most fluorescent light tubes also emit light in the ultraviolet range, although some do not. Sleeves can be purchased to slip over fluorescent tubes (see "Suppliers," Appendix 6), or fluorescent light

Fig. 2.6. The upholstery on the upper areas of this chair is noticeably paler in color than the upholstery protected from direct sunlight by the seat cushion.

fixtures can be replaced with fixtures that use incandescent bulbs. Always remain aware, however, that incandescent light bulbs, especially spot-lights, create damaging amounts of heat. Light bulbs can be prevented from harming a collection by use of heat filters or bulbs of low wattage, or by making certain that there is sufficient distance between the light source and the nearest artifact to prevent damage to the collection.

Measuring light levels. Light levels can be measured with devices called *photometers, luxmeters,* or *foot-candle meters.* A brief survey of these in-struments appears in Technical Bulletins Number 2, 3, and 7 of the Canadian Conservation Institute. Lighting levels are also discussed in G. Thomson's book *The Museum Environment.*

Light levels for furniture, paintings, and most other artifacts except those made of stone or metal should not exceed 150 lux (approximately 15 foot candles). For very sensitive materials, such as textiles and paper, light levels should be even lower—around 50 lux (approximately 5 foot candles).

Interior sides of windows may be retrofitted with ultraviolet shields of acrylic plastic (Plexiglas). The material can be purchased from plastics supply houses and may be cut to any size and fitted to frames made in a factory or in a local workshop. Smaller pieces may be fitted to panes of glass and held in place with glaziers' points. If that method is used, however, be sure that there is ample space between the Plexiglas and the window glass. I saw a historic house in farm country that had windows given that treatment, and dozens of flies, trapped in the space between the Plexiglas and the window glass, couldn't get out, creating a real problem. Also, thin self adhering plastic film can be applied directly to the glass. (See 3-M Company in supplier listing.) Note that the effectiveness of both film and Plexiglas decreases over time. Within three to four years, it is suggested the readings be taken with a UV light meter, as the materials may need to be replaced.

Mold—and How To Remove It

The appearance of mold among your artifacts is an indication that there are some things wrong in your environment. The principal causes are likely to be high humidity and poor air circulation.

Like cold germs, mold spores are present almost everywhere and are only waiting for the right conditions in the environment where a collection is housed to grow on wooden artifacts. In the presence of high humidity and stagnant air, mold spores will grow in areas where there is dirt, dust, and grease. The spores attack adhesives, paper, textiles, and other organic substances.

The first clue to the presence of mold is the odor of mildew. When you detect that odor, search around among your artifacts and you will find, somewhere in a neglected spot, a fluffy, scruffy growth, usually whitish, although it can be of any color.

Several procedures can kill the growing mold and, once it is eliminated, the conditions fostering it should be corrected to prevent a recurrence. Steps should be taken to achieve and maintain lower humidity and increased air circulation throughout the collection's environment. Isolate the mold-growing artifact from the rest of the collection, perhaps outdoors or in the garage. Brush off the mold growth and dispose of it in a

Fig. 2.7. A problem common to many collections is visible here: active mold growth on a dustcover.

plastic bag. There are numerous preparations that can be painted on the artifact's surface to kill the mold.

Someone once said to me, "Why don't you just wash off the mold?" What this observer failed to realize, however, was that the introduction of plain water to the organic material in a piece of furniture would simply encourage further mold growth, at an accelerated rate.

Use mineral spirits or turpentine to remove mold from a furniture finish. Make one pass over the surface with a cloth dampened—just *dampened*, not wet—with either solvent. Quickly dry the surface with a clean, dry cloth. Only if the mold is on an unfinished surface, such as the back or the inside of a piece, can the solvent be applied with a brush. After allowing the solvent to stand on the surface for a minute or two, dry it off with a clean, dry cloth.

Solvents other than benzine or turpentine may work better than they do at removing mold, but most of the others are hazardous and must be used in a spray booth or fume hood, so are not recommended.

One commercial prepartion that is useful for destroying mold on dust covers is "Lysol Regular" brand disinfectant—several other variations of the Lysol formula are available from the company producing it, but they contain ingredients not needed for our purposes here. Regular-strength Lysol disinfectant is made up of the following constituents:

Soap: 16.5 percent; o-phenylphenol: 2.8 percent; o-benzyl-p-chlorophenol: 2.7 percent; alcohols: 1.8 percent; xylenolds: 1.5 percent; isopropyl alcohol: 0.9 percent; and tetrasodium ethylenediamine tera-acetate: 0.9 percent.[2]

As with many commercial preparations, that one should be applied where there is good ventilation.

Another useful product for killing some forms of mold is, believe it or not, plain old mouthwash that contains a small percentage of thymol.[3] Heavier concentrations of thymol than are present in mouthwash are used as a mold killer only in laboratory situations. However, even the small amounts found in good, standard mouthwash that you can buy at the drugstore may be sufficient. Basic tests I've run all indicated that it would successfully eliminate mold. Following the tests, I applied the mouthwash to several pieces of upholstered furniture that had extensive mold growth on the dust covers. I brushed the fluid on in generous proportions, taking care not to get any on the furniture finishes, and the mold growth hasn't returned. *Do be very careful about keeping the mouthwash off furniture finishes; laboratory tests have indicated that mouthwash will cause a bloom on some finishes.*

Mothballs containing peradichlorobenzene will also kill mold. Place the moldy object in a plastic bag with a generous amount of mothballs. Before attempting the mothball treatment for mold, however, please refer to chapters 10 and 11 on infestation and safety procedures.

Dealing with moldy odors. Moldy odors commonly found inside furniture can be reduced with baking soda. Open a box of soda and leave it in a drawer or cupboard for two or three weeks, supported so that it won't fall over if the drawer or a cupboard door should suddenly be opened. If the odor persists, after two or three weeks, remove the old soda and put in a new box.

For extremely strong, offensive odors, such as that of a dead mouse hidden somewhere inside a piece of furniture, first remove the source of the odor; then sprinkle a thick layer of coconut charcoal on the offending spot and the surrounding area. If the odor is in a drawer, remove the drawer and seal it, with the charcoal, in a large plastic bag. Keep the drawer and the charcoal in the bag for several weeks; then, if traces of the odor remain, remove the old charcoal and put in a fresh supply.

❖ 3 ❖
Furniture Examination
Techniques

PROPER care of newly acquired furniture cannot begin until each piece has been thoroughly examined to determine what problems exist and decide what to do about them. Further, each piece that is already a part of your collection should be re-examined at regular intervals, to be sure that no new problems have developed undetected. If your artifacts have never been accessioned, the examination process provides an excellent opportunity for doing that; and it is also a good time to clean artifact surfaces not normally exposed or accessible. Further, when the basic examination of all pieces in the collection is completed, you will be in a better position to discuss priorities with a conservator or to do remedial treatments, yourself.

Procedure and Equipment

Examining furniture is not a simple task. It can be difficult for both the experienced and the inexperienced. Surveying a collection with numerous objects can be time-consuming and troublesome. Careful preparation can make the work much easier, however.

Before undertaking the job of examining a collection of furniture, design an all-purpose examination form to fit your own individual needs or special requirements. Fill out a form for each object examined. (Examples of conservators' forms are shown in Appendix 4.) Data recorded on the forms as the furniture is examined should be legible and systematic, and it should be stored in a permanent record file.

A proper location is essential for examining furniture. Space to be

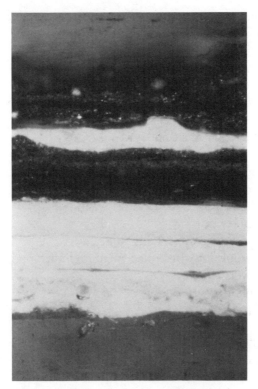

Fig. 3.1. Finishes of painted objects are usually more complex to repair than might be expected through superficial surface examination. Here, a photomicrograph of a painted object reveals what looks like a layer cake—at least eight layers of paint, concealed beneath the current finish.

used for the examination should be close enough to the furniture collection to allow easy movement of smaller objects to and from the collection and the examining site. The examination area should be away from the flow of traffic and free of casual visitors and other interruptions. Above all, there should be adequate illumination, preferably natural light, supplemented with movable electric lights.

With a workable form designed and a suitable location chosen, the next step toward examining the collection is to assemble the necessary tools and equipment. They include the following:

Note pad, pencils
Examination forms
Sawhorses (two pairs)
Examination table (one pair of sawhorses can be used for table legs under a 4-by-8-foot sheet of three-quarter-inch plywood)
Comfortable chair to sit on
Flashlight
Movable lights (mechanic's drop-light or one on a movable support)
Extension cord
Magnifying glass
Tape measure
Yardstick or carpenter's folding rule
Basic hand tools for wire replacement and mirror adjustments:
Screwdrivers
Adjustable wrench
Wire cutters
Awl
Padded movers' blankets
Padded blocks (see fig. 3.2)
Hand mirror
Mirror plate hangers
Assortment of brass screws for attaching hangers
Vacuum cleaner
Assorted sizes of paintbrushes for dusting
Dust cloths

If any information about the object being examined is available or is already on file, have that information close by for reference as you examine the piece, and note any comment made about the object's construction or condition. Especially important are earlier photographs.

To get into the swing of things, begin with pieces that are small and simple in construction. Once you've established a method of operation, you will be better prepared to tackle complex pieces.

Examine all pieces in detail. Smaller tables, chairs, lap desks, clocks, and so on can be moved to the examination table, turned over, moved about, and examined thoroughly. Larger pieces should be examined

Fig. 3.2. Padded blocks to support furniture for examination can be made by covering pieces of 2-by-4 lumber with carpet remnants.

where they stand, but more information can be gained by moving them a few inches out from the wall.

Moving and lifting. Be careful not to damage a piece in trying to move it, however; have plenty of strong help on hand and remember always to lift from the bottom, never by moldings, when you are handling case pieces. Before lifting *any* artifact, small or large, carefully examine its joints. Look for loose support elements, such as legs, and make sure that any part of the object that you are lifting by is secure.

Labeling for reassembly. Remove all drawers before turning over a piece. Look for signatures, labels, numbers, and so on, and record those that are found. Use chalk or small self-adhering labels to number each drawer on its unfinished bottom or back for proper reinstallation after examination. If self-adhering labels are used, be sure to remove them when the drawer is put back into place; if these labels are left on a piece of furniture, the adhesive on them may cause stains, or daubs of it may remain on the object. If examination discloses labels applied earlier, however, you may want to consider leaving them on, as part of the object's history. If you want to remove them, water applied with cotton may soften old adhesive residue and make it easier to remove from an unfinished surface. Mineral spirits or acetone may be required for some residues, but try water first. Before reinstalling the drawer, apply paste wax or paraffin to the runners to reduce abrasion. Examine for loose hardware and make a note of it, if any is found; then make whatever repairs are needed. On the permanent record form, record all repairs made and all materials used.

Recording measurements. Recording the measurements of each new piece examined is useful for identification purposes, and it is also helpful information to have at hand if the piece is to be transported or if it is to be fitted into an exhibition. Commonly used terms such as *width* and *length* mean different things to different people, and should be used only if necessary, such as when measuring a tabletop. To be most useful in working with furniture, measurements should specify the size of the piece *from side to side, from front to back,* and *in height.* All furniture measurements should be listed in inches, first, followed by measurement in centimeters, recorded in brackets. The examination form should show the largest dimension measured, because there will often be the difference of a fraction of an inch or so between one side of an object and the other. In measuring tables, make a notation on the form to show whether dimensions given indicate table leaves are up or down, whether a card table is open or closed, and so on.

Use a yardstick to find the front-to-back measurement of a chair. Place the back of the chair against a wall. With the chair facing you, insert the yardstick just below the front seat rail and ease the yardstick back until it hits the wall. For longer measurements, use a retractable tape measure, but make sure that the person holding the opposite end of the measure doesn't scratch the finish.

Use *proper* "left" and "right" sides: in measuring furniture, these designations are *respective to the object,* not to the viewer standing in front of the piece. For example, the "right" side of a chair is on *your* right when you are sitting on it; it will be on your *left* as you stand in front of the chair.

Examining mirrors. If there are mirrors in the collection being examined, check all hanger wires, screw eyes, and nail hangers in walls,

Fig. 3.3. Padded blocks support this mirror during examination.

and make any necessary repairs before rehanging the mirrors. Below are basic steps for mirror-testing, in proper sequence.

1. Remove the mirror from the wall, after checking to see that frame and glass are secure. Gently—but firmly—lift the mirror and place it on padded blocks against the wall.

2. Check the hanging device on the wall and, if it is loose, replace it. If the supporting nail is in plasterboard or plaster, replace the nail with a screw secured in a screw-anchor of plastic or lead.

3. Replace nonbraided wire with braided wire to provide necessary strength, duplicating the length of the old wire so that the mirror will hang at the same height as before.
4. If screw-eyes have been used to attach the hanging wire, remove the screw-eyes and replace them with mirror plate hangers.
5. Photograph the completed work; then rehang the mirror.

Accessioning. Accession numbers should be written legibly, as small as possible, and applied to an inconspicuous area on each collection piece, and the examination process is an ideal time for that. Insofar as possible, choose for placement of the accession number a location that will be in approximately the same place on each piece in the entire collection. That kind of planning in accession number placement can save a great deal of time, in the long run—considerable time may be wasted, later on, if one must search for accession numbers placed at random on each collection piece. The inconspicuous area selected for the accession number should be a place where the numbers can be read without moving the

Fig. 3.4. During examination of mirrors or paintings, check the hanging wire, screw eyes, and wall fasteners. Replace them, if necessary, with new wire, hangers, and wall fasteners such as those in the photograph.

object away from the wall—somewhere like the side of a rear leg, for instance, near the floor.

Neither clear nor colored nail polish should be used for applying the accession number to an area where a furniture finish is present. If a mistake is made or if the number has to be removed later for some other reason, the nail polish will have to be removed with acetone, which could also remove some of the piece's finish.

To apply accession numbers properly, purchase the following materials, and use them in the order listed:

1. Small paintbrush (for applying varnish)
2. Soluvar varnish (*Soluvar* is a trade name)
3. Fine-pointed paintbrush
4. Acrylic emulsion paint (white)

Use the small paintbrush to apply a base coat of Soluvar varnish to a spot just big enough to carry the accession number. Allow the varnish to dry. Use the fine-pointed brush and the acrylic emulsion paint to paint the accession number on, over the varnished spot prepared for it. Let the painted number dry. Seal the entire spot with a top coat of Soluvar varnish. Always be sure that each layer is dry before applying the next. The whole three-layer "sandwich" can be removed, later, if need be, with mineral spirits or turpentine.

Cleaning hidden surfaces. After the furniture has been examined, take the opportunity to clean furniture surfaces not usually exposed to view. Use the vacuum cleaner to remove cobwebs, dust balls, cocoons, and so forth, from areas brought to light during the examination. Wipe off all surface dust and dirt with a soft cloth. For further, intensive cleaning techniques, see chapter 8, on housekeeping, and chapter 4, on cleaning.

A Trial Run-Through, on Paper

For practice, we might run through an imaginary examination of a small veneered lap desk:

Step 1. Check the lap desk for any insecure part, such as a loose top. Gently lift the desk and carry it to the examination table. Look for evidence of insect powder—tiny bits of fine sawdust that tell you a wood-borer is at work.

Step 2. Turn the desk over, to look for any labels or handwriting that may be on the bottom. If anything of that sort is found, photograph it.

Fig. 3.5. Good lighting is necessary for any type of examination. Here, the examining room is darkened, and a light is held to one side of the small table being looked over. As the light rakes over the object's surface, the distortions in finish, veneer, and secondary structure become obvious.

Step 3. Record missing or broken elements.

Step 4. Tap on the veneer with a fingernail and listen for the hollow sound that cleft veneer makes. If you hear such a sound, note the location on the examination form.

Step 5. Examine the piece with raking light to note any bulges or dnts, over-all. If the piece has a painted surface, check for flaking or lifting paint. See figure 3.5 for an example of finish problems.

Step 6. Cover all categories on your form. If a few are not applicable to the piece you are examining, write "N/A" on the form.

Photographing the Collection

Photographs of each piece of furniture held should be part of the permanent files for a collection. Examination time is the ideal time to photograph newly acquired pieces. Additional photographs needed of the permanent stock may be made during survey time. Also, it is wise to photograph all pieces immediately before lending them to another institution or before packing them for transportation to an exhibition, in the event of damage during the transfer.

Not all conservators routinely furnish an entire series of photographs of all furniture under consideration, but most do provide relevant before-and-after-treatment photographs, upon request. Usually, a fee is charged for such photographs; sometimes the examination-and-treatment estimate includes the fee.

Should your collection be photographed in color or in black-and-white? Some conservators may take only black-and-white photographs; others favor color. I usually take black-and-white for recording conditions and treatments, but I also take color photos if color will be helpful in working with a particular object. For instance, color photographs may be necessary if the finish on a piece is badly bleached or deteriorated, or if the object has undergone bad restoration and it is obvious that considerable color change will take place when conservation treatment is completed. Each accession photograph should show the artifact's accession number and the date on which the photograph was made. In addition, I always include in the picture a simple, capital-letter code to indicate the current stage of treatment for the object. I use A to mean "Before treatment"; B is "During treatment," usually with late or improper repairs removed (*late repair* is any work done on the object since the original maker finished it); C means "During treatment," usually during various late stages of repair work; and D is "After treatment."

The accession number, photograph date, and any other information that might be useful if shown in the photograph can be included in the set-up by using magnetized numerals and letters, fitted into wooden holders that have been given a coat of metallic paint (see figure 3.6). Magnetized numerals and letters and metallic paint for finishing wooden holders that you make, as needed, are available from suppliers listed in Appendix 6. (Wooden holders are not available commercially.) These materials speed up the process of recording information on film considerably, if there are a good many objects to photograph. They also insure readability and make the photographic record look more professional than is possible with handwritten labels.

Fig. 3.6. Magnetic numbers are helpful in recording dates and identification numbers in photographs.

Large pieces of furniture should be photographed in place. Smaller ones can be set on a table top in front of a neutral, gray-colored backdrop.

If you hire someone to make pictures of your collection, stay with the photographer throughout the work session. The photographer's attention is going to be concentrated intently on the camera, on lighting, on the correct exposure, on focusing[1]—and the safety of other artifacts in or near the picture-taking area are *your* responsibility, as is the safety of the people in that area. Extension cords, cables, tripods, and lights are necessary parts of the photographer's paraphernalia; always be aware—and make others aware—of their locations, so that no one stumbles or trips over them, taking a fall and perhaps knocking them over, into other nearby equipment or artifacts.

The problem of hot lights. You may need to take other protective measures for artifacts too near the area where the photographs are being made. Photographic lights produce a great deal of heat—enough to damage nearby pieces of furniture or other objects sensitive to either light or heat. There are documented instances of artifacts being irrevocably scorched during photography sessions. One should also keep in mind that artifacts can even undergo thermal shock if they are brought directly from a cool environment into a hot photographic set-up.

Quartz halogen photographic lamps should be used for photographing artifacts, with heat-absorbing glass filters to absorb some of their heat output and mid-wave and short-wave ultraviolet radiation (below 400nm) as well. Electronic flash units and visible-light fluorescents should be used with plastic ultraviolet-absorbing filters. To minimize the risk of heat damage, ordinary tungsten incandescent photographic lamps as well as the filtered quartz halogen lamps should always be evenly spaced and placed about ten feet from the object to be photographed, so that there is a minimum heat transfer. A small fan can be used to circulate the warm air.

Flash bulbs should not be used in photographing artifacts, because the bulbs may shatter, hurling fragments of glass into objects—and people.

All photographic lamps should remain switched off, during a session, except when setting lights, determining exposure, and during actual exposure. Use of the lamps should be limited to periods lasting no longer than one minute at a time, because they can cause photodecomposition to take place if they are left on for more substantial periods of time, causing the materials of the artifacts to bleach or become brittle; and photodecomposition can continue, for a time, after the damaging light source is removed.

Total photography illumination, from all sources, should not exceed one hundred foot-candles (1,000 lux. *Lux* is an international unit of light measurement, signifying one *lumen* per square meter). Illumination of one hundred foot-candles should result in an exposure setting of about EV 9 at ASA 100 (that is, f/8 at 1/8 sec., or equivalent) when a reflectance reading is taken off a gray card or an incidence reading is taken with an incidence done on the meter.

For additional information on photographing collections, see D. Kushel's *Photodocumentation for Conservation: Procedural Guidelines and Photographic Concepts and Techniques*, published in 1980 by the American Institute for Conservation of Historic and Artistic Works; and see other publications in the bibliography.

X-Rays (Radiography)

Trained conservators can examine furniture through the use of radiography. Usually, conservators do not invest in X-ray equipment, but they may have access to it or may know where it is available.

Unfortunately, most pieces of furniture are too large or too awkward to be transported into the average medical radiography facility. However, conservation training institutions, some museum laboratories, and some conservation centers are involved in research of this kind.

Radiography facilities must be licensed and operated by highly skilled professionals. Excessive radiation exposure, devastating to humans, has no negative effect on artifacts. [2]

Radiographs can be confusing to a neophyte and may easily be misinterpreted by those not skilled in reading them. They should be analyzed by a conservator or a curator familiar with furniture construction and repair methods. Often, details of the original joinery, hidden by uphol-

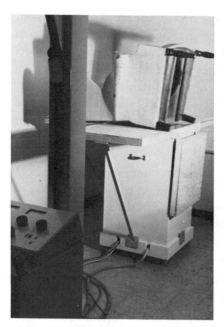 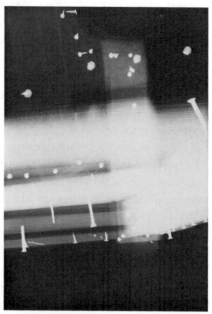

Fig. 3.7. An upholstered wing chair prepared for radiography.

Fig. 3.8. Radiograph (X-ray) of the wing chair shown in fig. 3.7 reveals the chair's hidden structure.

stery, are revealed in radiographs. Nails, upholstery tacks (see figure 3.8), and even early repairs are often discovered.

Ultraviolet Light

Like radiography, ultraviolet light (UV) examination can provide useful information to those skilled in its use. Small, hand-held ultraviolet examining units are available (see Appendix 6). Ultraviolet light provides information not seen with the naked eye and can cause the finish of an artifact to fluoresce differently in areas of repair. This is true of objects with transparent types of finishes, as well as painted objects. Findings should be discussed with a conservator who routinely uses this tool.

As with photographic lights, exposure time under ultraviolet examination should be limited, to reduce photodecomposition of the finish of the artifact.

❈ 4 ❈
Cleaning Dirty Furniture

D IRT on an artifact is not merely unsightly; it is a hazard that can seriously damage any surface, if it is allowed to remain and to accumulate. An accumulation of simple dust not only builds up an abrasive residue on fine furniture finishes; it attracts and holds moisture if the humidity runs high. Dirt is a breeding ground for mold. Built-up coatings of polish containing various oils and waxes can penetrate some furniture surfaces, carrying impurities, such as dust, with them.

With a collection that is kept clean, dusting finished surfaces once weekly is good practice. Sometimes it becomes necessary, however, to clean items that have accumulated more than the normal amount of household dust. That task is more complex than weekly dusting. Some precepts that can help in such instances follow.

Surface Cleaning

The first step in cleaning a piece of dirty furniture should be to go over it thoroughly but carefully with a vacuum cleaner. Before turning the vacuum on it, however, you need to examine the piece carefully, to be sure that there are no loose screws, no small, loose drawer pulls, peeling veneer, inlay, or pieces of molding that could be pulled off by the vacuum's suction. If you find anything even partially loose or not firmly attached, the best thing to do is to make it secure before you begin cleaning the piece.

If the object is very dirty, however, it may be desirable to run the vacuum over it *lightly* before securing those loose elements: otherwise, dirt may be trapped in recesses and under glued joints, and that can cause

Fig. 4.1. Close-up view of the underside of a table, where a visitor has deposited a lump of chewing gum.

more extensive work, later on. If it *is* necessary to clean with the vacuum before regluing, you can protect any fragile upholstery, paper labels, or drawers with wallpaper linings by making a screening device for the vacuum hose, to keep any small item from being sucked into the machine. Cut a piece of window screen approximately twelve inches square and cover the edges with masking tape or duct tape. Then, go ahead and vacuum the piece, holding the screen between the object and the vacuum's brush. A nylon stocking secured over the vacuum nozzle will also work.

As you run the vacuum over carvings, ledges, moldings, and recesses, brush the surface ahead of the nozzle gently with a soft paintbrush or a shaving brush. The brushing helps remove stubborn dirt particles from small cracks and crevices where it is hard to dislodge. Whenever you use these aids, be sure to keep the end of the vacuum cleaner nozzle at least

Fig. 4.2. Pieces of inlay that are beginning to lift, as is the small curved segment at left center, on this chest, are easy to snag in cleaning. Such loosening pieces of inlay should be reattached before the furniture is dusted or polished.

two or three inches away from all finished surfaces, and do not let the metal tip strike and damage the artifact being cleaned. Wrap masking tape around the nozzle to act as a bumper.

Never do more than vacuum and dust interior surfaces, cabinet backs, backs of doors, and bottoms of drawers and compartments. Never apply abrasives, solvents, or cleaning solutions to these areas; here the experienced individual begins the examination. These ordinarily unseen surfaces are rarely tampered with when a piece is restored, and they can provide a wealth of historical information in the form of old tool marks, signatures, makers' notations, and types of finishes used. For example, we treated a Windsor settee that had been completely stripped and refinished some time before. We were delighted to discover, however, that the entire history of the various finishes applied to the piece could be seen on the bottom, where at least four colors of paint were visible.

After vacuuming superficial dirt, you will have a better view of what remains and the next step can be more effectively planned.

Fig. 4.3. White outlines at the lower left corner of this piece of furniture show clearly where pieces of decorative wood inlay have loosened and disappeared. Fortunately, the inlay pieces were stored properly, after becoming detached.

Heavier Cleaning; Treating Disfigurement

For heavier cleaning, always begin with the mildest methods and materials, to retain what patina the finish of the piece may have. Never remove anything that shows evidence of the object's functional use: cupboard doors often show dark stains along the opening and closing edges, from decades of imprints made by greasy fingers. Tool handles exhibit the same type of patina. Stains from the lubrication of moving parts fall into this category: spinning wheels, for instance, often have dark stains near bearing surfaces.

Such objects as spinning wheels, pie safes, and many kinds of tools would ordinarily no longer be in use as functional objects; therefore, any

Fig. 4.4. The side piece at the top of this wooden cradle shows checking and protrudes slightly out of plane. All points considered, the safest treatment is to leave the cradle in this condition. Simply nailing it up flush would put additional stress on the structure, resulting in a continuation of the check. The cleaning staff should be advised of its condition.

newly acquired grime on them from handling is disfigurement. To clean such recent marks, use the following procedures:

1. Find an inconspicuous area on the object that needs cleaning, and test the finish carefully with various cleaning liquids. This is essential, to find out what should or should not be used. To test the finish, dampen a cotton-tipped applicator—a Q-tip—with distilled water to which has been added one teaspoon of detergent per gallon of water (see "Suppliers," in Appendix 6). Gently rub the dampened applicator over a small area of the test space. The applicator should pick up surface grime without softening the finish. After the test area dries for a few minutes, make sure that the finish isn't going to whiten. A white discoloration— called *bloom*—indicates that moisture is penetrating the finish and, perhaps, remaining permanently.

2. If there is no bloom in the test area, fill a bucket with distilled

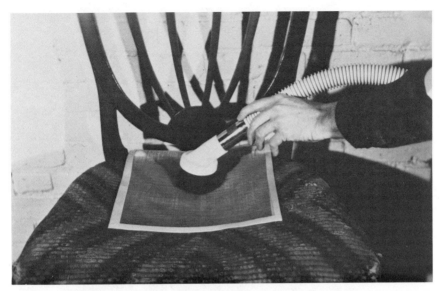

Fig. 4.5. The first step in cleaning a dirty piece of furniture is to go over it with a vacuum cleaner. A small piece of screen wire, the kind used for window screens, with all edges carefully covered by masking tape, can be held between the end of the vacuum hose wand and the furniture, to keep fragments of wood or fabric from being sucked up into the vacuum.

water that is at room temperature. For each gallon of water, add one teaspoonful of the detergent that has been proven safe in the applicator testing.

3. Dampen a clean sponge with the water; place the sponge inside a towel and wring it almost dry. *Do not use a wet sponge, because you do not want excess water to remain on the artifact's surface.* Work in small areas with the damp sponge, and don't rub too hard.

4. Dry the sponged area with soft towels, warmed *very* slightly in an oven, to absorb any moisture from the surface. A hot plate may also be used to warm drying towels, but hold the towels far enough above the heating element to prevent any chance of their catching fire.

5. After initial cleaning and drying, go over the object again, with a different clean sponge dampened in a bucket of fresh, clean water—and, again, the sponge should be wrung nearly dry in a towel—to remove any detergent residue from the cleaning process.

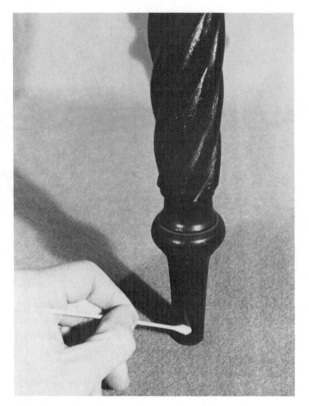

Fig. 4.6. Test the reaction to cleaning fluids on a finished wooden surface in an inconspicuous place by rolling over the test spot a cotton-tipped applicator dampened in the cleansing solution you plan to use.

Solvents—Pro and Con

If surface grime still remains on the artifact, or if you wish to remove wax build-up, further cleaning is possible, although that will involve using solvents—a step that must be taken very carefully. Although some solvents are safe on many finishes, there are always exceptions; and improper use of solvents can overclean or remove a finish. Many times, overcleaning will damage a beautiful and secure patinated finish.

Solvents can also prove injurious to the people working with them, if proper safety measures are not followed. Before beginning a job using solvents, see chapter 11, "Health Hazards and Safety Practices."

Fig. 4.7. Localized bloom shows in whitish areas on a wooden surface. This example of it was caused in testing a piece of furniture with a cotton-tipped applicator. When the fluid being tested causes such a blemish, discontinue its use at once and find another solution or solvent.

At the risk of overemphasizing the point, I would stress, again and again: *Always be conservative when cleaning an entire piece of furniture.* Never scrub too hard; you may risk making some areas lighter than others. Before you undertake rigorous, over-all cleaning, let the piece sit for a few days; then consider the artifact in its entirety before reaching for strong cleaning solutions. Chances are, the spot you once considered incongruous will appear as a beauty-mark.

True Grime—and Some Safer Solvents

Relatively safe solvents for removing grime are benzine and turpentine. Odorless paint thinner may be substituted—it has no objectionable odor, which gives it an advantage over other solvents. However, the use of all these relatively safe solvents has in some instances resulted in whitening some finishes, so—*always*—test, first. Obviously, one must use these solvents—and any others worked with—only where there is good ventilation, where there are no electrical sparks from running motors and no open flames from pilot lights or gas heaters. Solvents are highly flammable substances, and vapor from them can be ignited from any spark or live flame.

As in lighter, surface cleaning, test the solvent you plan to use for heavy-duty cleaning on the object to be cleaned by dampening a cotton-tipped applicator in the full-strength solution. Press out most of the solvent and roll the dampened swab over a small, obscure area of the artifact. Too much solvent slows down evaporation and can soften the finish below the grime and wax. Immediately dry the area with a soft, clean rag. Let any remaining solvent evaporate for an hour or so and again check for whitish discoloration—called *blanching* (see glossary) when caused through use of a solvent—before you go any further.

If your choice of solvents performs satisfactorily in the test procedure and does not harm the finish, you have three materials to choose from for applying it: a piece of cloth, pieces of cotton, or No. 4/0 (0000) steel wool. Steel wool can cause the most damage, if abused. If used properly, however, No. 4/0 steel wool can be useful for removing a thick layer of grime or wax build-up. *Never* use steel wool rated 1/0 (0), 2/0 (00), or 3/0 (000)—they are all far too coarse for a furniture finish. The use of steel wool is necessary if the surface is going to have a new finish applied. After cleaning with solvents, dry the surface with a cloth. The piece should then be ready for waxing or refinishing.

Cleaning Marble Tops, Piano Keys, and Leather Surfaces

For routine cleaning of marble tops only, use a vacuum cleaner with a brush attachment. Do not dust marble tops with a cloth; that tends to smear grime over the surface and press it down into the porous stone. Do not apply any type of cleaning solution on marble, including soap or detergents, so that it covers the entire surface. Any liquid used may actually carry foreign material deeper into the stone, creating a stain or leaving a deposit that may discolor the piece.

To remove localized grime from marble, don a pair of rubber gloves; dip a wad of cotton into a 5 percent solution of clear household ammonia in distilled water; wring out most of the fluid and apply the dampened cotton to the soiled area. Follow with an application of distilled water, also applied with a wrung-out wad of cotton. Then lay a soft cloth on top of the area—*don't rub*—to absorb moisture.

Ivory piano keys can also be cleaned with the methods used for marble tops, *but be aware that no guarantee accompanies any of these suggestions.*

Removing stains from leather surfaces is an especially tricky business. I hesitate recommending the use of leather dressings, as the leather surface may have already been impregnated with numerous coatings of oils, waxes, and various commerical products, some containing silicone; therefore, introducing a new compound to the surface may create a mess or a bloom. However, if a leather surface is disfigured by real grime that must be removed, or if you need to make a leather surface more uniform, use the following procedure—always remembering to test in an obscure area first with a cotton-tipped applicator.

First, stir into a quart of distilled water at room temperature a tiny bit of saddle soap, about the size of a pea. After that dissolves, and after you've tested it in a small, back area of the artifact, dampen a cloth in the solution and wipe it over the leather surface several times. Follow by wiping the surface with another cloth dipped in plain distilled water, to pick up the soap residue. Blot the surface dry with a soft, clean, dry cloth and allow the piece to dry overnight.

At that point, you might want to apply a leather dressing containing anhydrous lanolin and neat's-foot oil—but first, read pages 43–64 of Carolyn Horton's *Cleaning and Preserving Bindings and Related Materials,* second edition (Chicago: American Library Association, 1969). A leather dressing should be used only on smooth, sound material, and *no leather dressing should be used without first being tested on each individual piece of leather.*

⭐ 5 ⭐
Wooden Elements:
Repair and Replacement

A FTER a newly acquired piece of furniture has been examined, accessioned, photographed, and cleaned, the logical protective measures to take next are to assess whatever damage there may be and make decisions on what to do about all loose, detached, or missing parts—and this is a good place to say the following, which is valid not only here, but throughout every chapter in this book.

Furniture can be constructed of several types of woods. The larger the variety of woods used in a piece, the more complex the entire structure becomes. It is not uncommon to see inlaid surfaces consisting of several types of woods, each with a different rate of expansion and contraction. Textiles, leather, metals (ferrous and nonferrous), glass, stone, and ivory can also be used, in addition to different kinds of woods, in making furniture. All of these materials can be covered with a variety of finishes, including paint, lacquer, varnish, shellac, wax, plaster, gesso, bole, and metal leaf. And all of those substances react to the same environment in different ways, so that they must be dealt with as individual objects for the safety and integrity of the whole.

The computer at the Smithsonian Institution Conservation Analytical Laboratory was once asked this question: Given the number of materials commonly found in furniture, how many job skills should a furniture conservator have? The answer the computer came up with was "More than 150."[1]

This book would swell to more than ten times its present size if I went into specifics about ways to replace missing elements from all of the above categories. Even then, no one could become proficient in the requisite skills by simply reading a book.

One individual who read a draft of this work in manuscript remarked that, since not everyone could afford a conservator, the book should teach a museum carpenter how to become a furniture conservator. However, as the reader knows, by now, our purpose here is to point out workable ways in which collectors, curators, or skilled carpenters with limited funds can properly care for furniture in their collections. It also points out areas where people *can* do *some* remedial work and where those trained in cabinetmaking can follow through with more advanced work.

Separations—Detached Elements—and Their Repair

Old furniture is vulnerable to loss of detached elements of three general kinds: detached or cleaving veneer or inlay; separation of applied wooden elements such as molding or carvings; and structural joint separation, which is what happens when a chair-back or a leg has either come off or has been subjected to so much wear and tear that it has become ineffectual at the point where it joins another element.

Systematic analysis of the problem and careful preparation before starting work are essential in dealing with all three kinds of separations.

First—and this is especially necessary if the object has been on the premises for some little time since its examination on arrival—check the piece over, to be sure that it is clean. If it has sat long enough to accumulate a fresh coating of dust and dirt, it should be freshly cleaned. Then, the tools and equipment needed for that particular job should be assembled.

Cleaving Veneer and Inlay

Wood veneers and inlays are attached to furniture for decorative purposes. Inlays consist of numerous materials, including wood, metal, shell, bone, horn, and various other things. Thin layers of these materials cover the more substantial, structural elements of many pieces of furniture, and cleavage can develop as the different components pull apart.

A frequent cause of cleavage in veneer and inlay is fluctuation in

Fig. 5.1. A knowledge of numerous materials is necessary for the furniture conservator. The detail shown here of one piece of furniture reveals five substances—paint, metal, paper, shell, and wood—used within just a few square inches.

humidity. High humidity causes adhesives between the veneer or inlay and the secondary structure below to absorb moisture and become soft. On the other hand, low humidity makes the adhesives brittle. Either condition can cause damage.

In addition, the rates of expansion and contraction of the thin decorative layers are different from those of the secondary structure as moisture is taken in and given off.

As may be imagined, these conditions lead to separations of the different materials. Cleavage of veneer and inlay is more apparent in winter, when heated environments dry out adhesives, and wood loses a high percentage of its moisture content.

Cleavage may also develop during shipment, as the traveling furniture tries to reach an equilibrium with its new environment.

Lifting or blistered veneer and inlay can be spotted easily when one visits a collection housed in an uncontrolled environment. Ends of brass

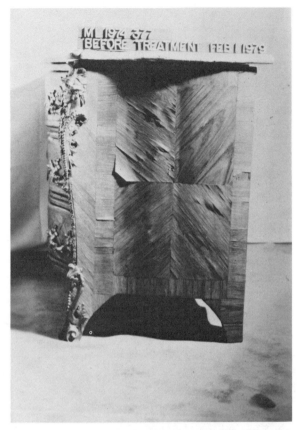

Fig. 5.2. The common problem of veneer cleavage is clearly visible on this three-drawer French commode.

banding in such an environment also commonly pop off, to become appendages waiting to snag a passerby. After being pulled off, such tentacles are too often simply gathered and stuck away in drawers with the best of intentions for later reattachment. Unfortunately, they are frequently not labeled and are eventually very likely to be thrown out during some overzealous housecleaning.

Before veneer or inlay cleavage reaches the separation point, however, it can be detected in time to correct it with no location problems. Simply tap a veneered area with a fingernail and listen for a hollow sound. When I examine a veneered or inlaid piece, I go over the surface,

Fig. 5.3. Here is the same French commode shown
in fig. 5.2—*after* treatment for cleaving veneer.

tapping, to assess the extent of possible incipient cleavage. Later, just before
the re-gluing procedure, I go over the entire surface again and mark each
area of cleavage with a small piece of masking tape (see fig. 5.5). To get the
small squares of tape, I attach a larger piece of tape to a piece of Plexiglas,
then use an X-Acto knife (or equivalent) to cut the tape into pieces approximately 1/4 of an inch square. I mark each area where separation of
veneer is detected by pulling off a small square of tape from the Plexiglas
backing and attaching it to the endangered area. The masking-tape marker
should not be left on more than a few days, as it can damage a finish.

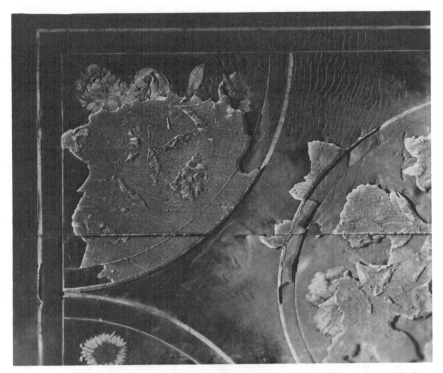

Fig. 5.4. Detail of this piece reveals missing areas of inlay, unfortunately lost long ago, before anyone took an interest in the total object.

To reattach separations in veneer or inlay, you will need, first, to select a clean work area with a relative humidity of 35 percent to 70 percent; below or above that range, your adhesives will not harden properly. Then you will need to assemble these pieces of equipment:

1. One or two syringes
2. Warm water, in a pan
3. Bottle of hide glue (see Appendix 6)
4. Bottle of distilled water
5. Several clean cloths
6. Several small pieces of 1/8-inch-thick Plexiglas of various sizes (about 1 by 2 inches, 2 by 4 inches, and so on), with all edges and corners sanded smooth
7. Clamps (wooden cam-action clamps of various sizes are mentioned in Appendix 5)
8. Table, stool

Fig. 5.5. When a piece of furniture appears likely to have numerous areas of veneer cleavage, go over it thoroughly, tapping the surface with a fingernail and listening for the hollow sound made by cleaving veneer. With a small piece of masking tape, mark each area to be repaired.

9. Movers' blanket
10. Wax paper
11. Throat atomizer
12. Spring-loaded curtain rods with rubber tips (fig. 5.5)
13. Masking tape

With all equipment assembled, you are ready to start. Follow these steps:

1. Position the object for the work to be done. If you need to turn the piece over, place it on a movers' blanket protected by wax paper on a bench or on sawhorses.

2. Place the bottle of glue in a pan of warm water before you begin work; warmed glue is easier to work with. Cool and at full strength, hide glue is too viscous to pass through most needles. Manufacturers also recommend that hide glue be used at 72 degrees Fahrenheit or above during any application process.

3. With a syringe, inject distilled water under the area of separation. A throat atomizer can also be used, in areas where the separation is wide enough to accommodate it. The injection of water will usually soften the old existing glue, as water-soluble glues were used in the construction of early furniture.

4. Wipe up any excess water.

5. Clamp the soaked area with a piece of Plexiglas for one minute. If your clamp won't reach, you may be able to use a weight, a curtain rod, or a tourniquet. A curtain rod can also be used as a type of veneer press.

6. Empty the syringe of water—or use a second syringe—and fill it with warm hide glue. It is important to return the syringe to the warm water in the pan where the glue bottle is, to keep the system working.

Fig. 5.6. The best way to get glue under an area of cleaving veneer is to use a syringe.

Fig. 5.7. Spring-loaded curtain rods are useful for applying pressure to areas where clamping would be difficult. A small strip of Plexiglas distributes the pressure evenly and safely.

7. Inject the glue, wipe up the excess, and clamp the spot with Plexiglas, as before. It may be necessary to remove the clamp and the Plexiglas once or twice, because additional glue may be pressed out. In addition to distributing pressure, the Plexiglas allows the object's surface to remain visible, which is helpful, as it may be necessary to adjust the veneer under the clamp.

8. After the glue has dried for twenty-four to forty-eight hours, re-move the clamp. The Plexiglas may have stuck to the surface, but a gentle push from one side should pop it loose.

9. Excess glue can be wiped off the surface with a damp cloth.

Adhesives for Mending Separations

For repairing separations in veneer and inlay, an adhesive should be used that will combine sufficient strength with ease of reversibility— requirements necessary for two reasons: first, a really strong adhesive

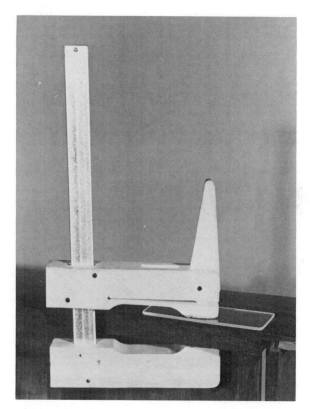

Fig. 5.8. A wooden cam-action clamp provides gentle pressure for veneered surfaces. The Plexiglas strip placed between the clamp and the wood surface distributes pressure over a larger area, allows you to see the surface being treated, and keeps the clamp from adhering to the veneer. After the adhesive dries—in twenty-four to forty-eight hours—remove the clamp. The Plexiglas may be stuck to the surface, but a gentle push from the side will dislodge it.

could cause the veneer to split as the wood below it expands at a rate different from that of the veneer; second, the adhesive should be reversible, so that if it becomes necessary to replace, modify, or adjust the repairs later on, that can be done by injecting water, without damaging the surrounding materials.

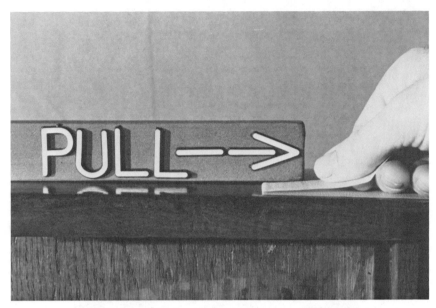

Fig. 5.9. If you don't have the proper wooden cam-action clamps for repairing veneered surfaces, small areas with minor cleavage can be held down with reinforced mailing tape or masking tape. After the adhesive dries—for twenty-four to forty-eight hours—remove the tape by pulling it straight back, so that you don't pull up your fresh repair along with the tape. A piece of Plexiglas can also be used to isolate the repair area.

It is easy to find a commercial glue stronger than the wood itself. However, thin veneer and inlay materials take up and give off proportionately greater amounts of moisture than their thicker supports.[2] They have enough inherent problems, without compounding their difficulties, and a weak adhesive that simply lets go (cleaves) at the joint is desirable. Inevitably, you will have to reglue that area, in the future, but at least the delicate inlay will remain whole. Commercial liquid hide glue qualifies as a good glue for these jobs, because it is strong enough without being too strong, and it is easily reversible.

Animal-hide glue. Animal-hide glues, used since ancient times, are prepared commercially from animal products—usually cattle by-products—and the raw materials may contain hooves, bones, and connective tissue, as well as hides. The raw animal matter is washed with water, then cured with milk of lime—a suspension of calcium hydroxide or hydrated lime in water—for removal of non-glue proteins. The stock is then treated with acids, rinsed with water, and cooked for glue extraction. Chemically, animal glue is a polydisperse system containing molecules of numerous weights. It is also a protein derived from hydrolysis of collagen.[3]

Professional cabinetmakers and conservators sometimes still use the hot hide glue found on early furniture. Its use is ethical, and it has both strength and reversibility, but experience is required to mix and use it properly.

Yellow emulsion glue. Yellow emulsion glue, a variety of polyvinyl acetate emulsion, could also be used in working with separations; it is especially useful for reattaching support elements. Research indicates that yellow emulsion glue adhesion lines will soften on exposure to water and that they maintain their strength in both low humidity and high humidity. Being gap-filling and elastic, they are well suited for ill-fitting joints. These yellow aliphatic glues can—at least, theoretically—be redissolved with water. [4]

White emulsion glues. White emulsion glues should not be used on furniture. White emulsion glues have been widely used since World War II, but their reversibility is questionable. White polyvinyl acetate emulsion glues were introduced as a synthetic resin substitute for hide glue. Being less viscous than the yellow emulsions, they penetrate more deeply, making it impossible to remove them later. Also, if some of this glue flows onto the surface of a piece of furniture, it will create a finish barrier that may be impossible to remove for any subsequent localized refinishing.

Separations of Moldings and Other Wooden Elements

A second category of separations includes moldings, carvings, and applied wooden elements. It is important, in repairing these elements, not to modify or try to improve any original material. In addition, under no circumstances should a separated wooden element ever be reattached with nails and screws if such fasteners were not used originally. New nails and screws have severely damaged many pieces of old furniture. Not only are they hard to remove, but—like a too-strong adhesive—they also restrict natural movement of wood, resulting in new splits or checks.

The edges of moldings and applied elements usually have notable traces of finish, grime, wax, and so on. It is best not to remove these

Fig. 5.10. Never restrict the movement of wood by adding nails or screws where they were not used originally. Probable results of such "fixing" are shown here.

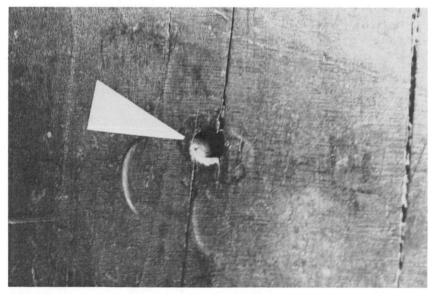

Fig. 5.11. The arrow points to a common mishap on this piece of furniture: not only did the nails driven into it restrict wood movement, resulting in clearly evident checks, but the perpetrator missed the mark with the hammer, leaving visible dents in the wood.

encrustations, because the clean edges left where they join other elements would make the repair work stick out like a sore thumb.

For reattaching these ornamental elements, use hide glue—but only if the element being repaired was glued, before. Apply the glue either by injection or with a brush, following the same procedures as used for repairing veneer and inlay.

If original or early nails or screws are present in pieces of molding or carving, use them for reattachment, instead of using glue. Try to match them to their original holes. If they no longer fit and do not function as fastening devices because of worn threads, wooden plugs can be inserted in the holes and the old screws can be inserted into the plug. Begin with an oversize dowel. Shave it down with a knife or rasp, so that its sides are irregular and not perfectly round. Apply yellow emulsion glue and press the plug into the hole. Cut off the new plug level with the surface and let the glue around it dry. When the glue is dry, drill an undersized hole in the center of the new plug and make a proper pilot-hole in it for the old screw.

Fig. 5.12. Loose screws are a common problem in furniture restoration, but all hardware found in old furniture should be retained, especially if it is early—or, even, possibly the original hardware.

Figs. 5.13, 5.14, 5.15, 5.16, 5.17, and 5.18. To correct the problem of loose screws in a hinge, begin by taking out the screws and removing the hinge (fig. 5.13). Then select an oversized dowel or a piece of wood approximately the size of the old screw-hole. Shave down the dowel sides so that the wood is not perfectly round and will fit snugly in the screw-hole (fig. 5.14). Apply yellow emulsion or hide glue to the holes and tap in the dowel plugs (fig. 5.15). Use side-cutters to cut the ends of the plugs off flush with the surface of the door (fig. 5.16). Allow the glue to dry; then drill new screw-holes approximately the size of the smallest diameter of the screw. A push drill, with bits of various sizes, is a useful tool for this (fig. 5.17). The hinge can now be reattached, and the glued-in wooden plug gives the old screw new purchase so that it will hold firmly (fig. 5.18).

Nails can be squeezed or pressed in with a framer's fitting tool, such as that shown in chapter 6 (fig. 6.10) or they can be tapped into place with a soft hammer. A block of wood or a dowel between the head of the hammer and the nail head will prevent denting the surface of the wood. For screws that need to be replaced, see chapter 6, "Metal Elements."

Structural Joint Separation

Structural joint separations include both secondary and primary elements. Tools and equipment for repairing structural separations are the same as those needed in working with veneers and inlays, with the exception of the glues. With structural joint separation, too, reversibility is important when choosing an adhesive. However, correcting joint separations requires a glue with more strength than commercial liquid hide glue provides, especially when the separation is in a support element, such as a leg. The hot hide glue of the early furniture makers can be used, so long as an experienced person mixes and applies it; and yellow emulsion glue is also good. You will also want to have on hand a wax-paper cone for applying the glue (see figs. 5.19 and 5.20), clamps, and a paintbrush of the size needed—in a width of one, two, or three inches—with stiff bristles, to apply the adhesive to the joint surfaces.

If the loose element is separated entirely, don't scrape off any of the remaining scraps of old glue. Soften them, instead, by brushing on water—unless a previous repair at that spot was done with an adhesive not soluble in water. It is necessary to maintain the spacing created by the old adhesive. As with repairs to molding separations, be careful not to remove visible material near the edges, where the finish has built up or accumulated.

In working with joint separations, follow the procedures outlined for replacing veneer. In reattaching joint separations, however, additional clamps, such as bar clamps, may be necessary. If so, use them with caution, and pad the area where the clamp contacts the object, since bar clamps can easily damage a surface if tightened excessively. Above all, don't try to modify the joining surfaces if they do not match perfectly. To modify joinery is a complex operation that one should undertake only as a last resort, after considering all the alternatives.

Also—if, after you re-glue a chair, you notice that one leg does not touch the floor, *do not attempt to correct it.* It's quite possible that long

5.19

5.20

Figs. 5.19 and 5.20. One simply made and effective tool for repairing joint separations is a cone shaped from wax paper and filled with hide glue. The cone is then squeezed to inject the adhesive. The applicator tip on a commercial adhesive bottle can also be used.

5.21

5.22

Figs. 5.21 and *5.22*. Before treatment (fig. 5.21), the reverse side of this wooden chest shows large horizontal checks that allow dust to enter the piece. To repair the damage (fig. 5.22), strips of linen are attached with hide glue, covering the cracks and allowing the surrounding wood to expand and contract with minimal restriction.

years of wear and tear had already loosened the joinery and abraded the leg ends until that leg wasn't the same length as the other three, anyway. This hands-off principle is even more important if the chair is to be returned to a historic house. Why tamper with one historic chair leg to make all four feet sit squarely, when the floor they will be sitting on may be, itself, distorted?

Never try to improve on the original joinery, primitive though it may be; to do that would also be to compromise the object's integrity.

If necessary, shims can fill gaps; and glue can have fine sawdust added. Sawdust makes the glue serve as a filler, although it reduces glue's adhesive qualities. On the other hand, the aggregate of sawdust particles acts to arrest tiny cracks that might develop later, should the filler material become brittle.

In all work with joint separations, make sure that, by gluing, you are not creating additional stresses and restricting natural expansion and contraction. For example, see figs. 5.21 and 5.22, showing splits in the back board of a chest. If we close the gaps by clamping and gluing, we are introducing a restrictive mechanism, since there was no glue in that area before. As the photograph shows, to prevent the entry of dust, linen strips were attached in place with commercial hide glue, allowing the wood to fluctuate.

Missing Parts: Replacement Techniques

There are two valid approaches to the question of replacing parts missing from old furniture: one suggests that when elements or parts of elements of an artifact are missing, those parts should be replaced with materials that correspond to the original as closely as possible, both in appearance and composition; the other holds that, when an element is missing, it should be replaced with another element that is an obvious replacement. For example, if a foot were missing from a small decorative object in a museum collection, it might be replaced with a Plexiglas support. That is a valid approach: it is an honest interpretation for the museum viewer. While I have used that approach, on rare occasions, I should prefer, usually, to make the replacement part as much a replica of the original as possible, so that the entire object is once again whole. I feel that my replacement parts should not disfigure the original maker's intent, but should blend with the over-all concept of the piece.

Figs. 5.23, 5.24, and *5.25.* A highchair in need of replacement parts: a large segment of the crest rail (see detail, fig. 5.24) and the entire stretcher are missing. Broken-off pieces of furniture, such as the end of the crest rail missing here, should always be saved and stored properly. Fig. 5.25 shows the repair finished, with reconstructed elements properly in place.

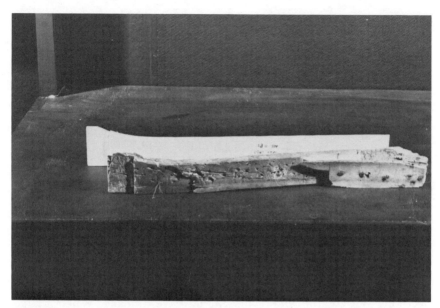

Fig. 5.26. The new part fabricated to replace a structural piece as a sofa was being stabilized is shown here alongside the old part. The new element was clearly marked with the name of the individual who made the replacement, the date of repair, and the place where the work was done.

As a general precept, however, when it comes to reproducing missing elements, that work is best left to the professional conservator. A conservator's repairs, while not obvious to the average museum viewer, *should* be obvious when the piece undergoes analysis. A large replacement part can be readily identified by a signature on the underside. The conservator's name or that of the institution owning the artifact should be given, as well as the location of the institution and the date (see fig. 5.26).

Obviously, the signature approach should be limited only to large parts. Numerous veneer losses can be documented through "before" and "after" photographs, as should any other repair work. One idea that I heard of suggested placing a tiny chip of aluminum foil under each new piece of veneer put in, so that replacements could then be identified through radiography.

Materials: Originals or Synthetics?

It would be impossible—or illegal—to reproduce some missing parts out of the same material as that of the original, unless the conservator had a long-standing supply of such materials stashed away. Included among such sensitive materials are tortoise shell and ivory (from endangered species). These materials can be reproduced synthetically, so that filling voids with a similar-looking substance is often done in conservation laboratories. That approach to the problem is completely ethical, so long as everything involved in such a procedure is documented.

Sometimes, missing parts are cast in a mold made from existing pieces. For a conservator or a cabinetmaker to reproduce complex decorative elements out of wood would not be impossible, but it would be very time-consuming. Decisions about whether it may be worthwhile to devote a great deal of time to making a replacement part out of the same kind of material as the original or whether it would be more practical to use other materials and methods that would get the job done faster are decisions that curators and owners would have to make. When a large replacement part is needed for a wooden artifact, the decision commonly made is to cast a new part, with the proper documentation. That is a valid and ethical approach; and it should be used when the missing part is for decorative purposes and will not be used to support weight or to hold the structure together. A complex applied element such as a quadrifoil can be cast by making an impression of an existing model in plasteline— a nonhardening modeling clay. A small amount of Titebond glue should first be stirred into a cup of water. Durham's Rock-Hard Water Putty is then added in the proportions suggested on the container. The putty is poured into the plasteline mold and allowed to harden overnight. The hard new piece is then removed from the mold and finished to match the original. It is then attached with liquid hide glue. (All of the products mentioned here are available from suppliers listed in Appendix 6.)

Replacing Losses in Veneer

In working with veneer, most losses should not be filled with anything but another piece of veneer. Fills in veneer made from a foreign material never look right and often cause problems if they have to be removed. The only exceptions are small voids and cracks in veneered surfaces that can be bridged with a filler.

The correct process in replacing veneer losses involves identifying the type of wood from which the original was made and then substituting a new piece made from the same kind of wood, with a similar figure. Stain tests for the new strip should be made on a large piece of the new veneer, near an edge. Tests should not be made on the small area that will eventually be transferred to the artifact; that area is left alone until an appropriate color match is made. Finishes, such as shellac, sanding sealer, or lacquer are also tried over the test spots, as they can also change the color of the new veneer.

When the match is satisfactory, the stain and the finish are applied to the small area with the similar figure, on the bench, before attachment. A rubbing is made on the artifact, to get the exact configuration of the missing area. The shape needed for the replacement can be cut out of the paper used for the rubbing and attached with a water-soluble adhesive over the new veneer, or it can be traced onto the new veneer with carbon paper. The new finished piece, cut out by hand with a jewelers' saw or a scroll saw (see Appendix 6) fitted with a jewelers' fine-toothed

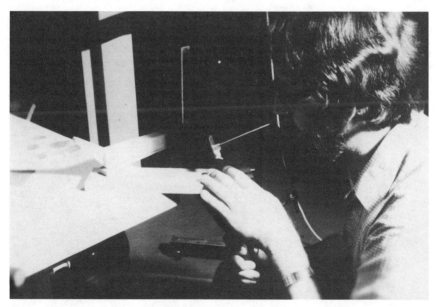

Fig. 5.27. Conservation Intern Rick Sherin reproduces missing segments of veneer.

Fig. 5.28. Properly shaped veneer replacement pieces are made by tracings and/or rubbings.

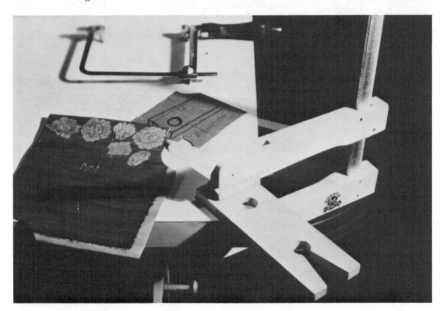

Fig. 5.29. Some common tools used in veneer replacement.

saw blade, is finally set in place with hide glue and clamped with the same techniques used to correct veneer cleavage.

Paint Losses

Paint losses are rarely replaced with the same type of paint as the original medium, because the older paint was usually based on a drying oil (see chapter 7). Usually, conservators repair paint losses by inpainting with pigments ground in a synthetic medium that is easily reversible.

Fig. 5.30. The small inserts visible here on close inspection represent an "honest" repair. Early repairs often add character to an object and are part of its history. So long as they do not add instability or considerable disfigurement, they should be retained.

⬦ 6 ⬦
Metal Elements and Metal Leaf:
Repair and Replacement

URNITURE hardware includes both utilitarian and ornamental elements. Hinges, locks, latches, drawer pulls, and door handles—and the nails and screws that hold them in place—serve utilitarian functions. Escutcheons, mounts, finials, and things of that sort—and *their* fasteners—are applied decorative parts whose primary function is to add embellishment. Inlaid metal is not included in this

Fig. 6.1. Detail of mount on a French desk.

Fig. 6.2. A large French two-drawer commode with numerous gold-plated bronze mounts, shown here before treatment. The commode's heavy marble top—not present in the photograph—was left on site, rather than risk damage to it as the piece was transported for repair.

Fig. 6.3. The same French two-drawer commode shown in fig. 6.2, *after* treatment.

category, as replacement work with it should follow practices discussed for other inlaid materials, in the early pages of chapter 5.

As a newly acquired piece of furniture is being given the thorough initial cleaning it should have, an appropriate part of the initial work is to determine the kind of metal present on the artifact. A conservator can analyze the metal material in a laboratory. Using proper sampling techniques, a microscope, and appropriate reagents, conservators need only a negligible amount of sample material to determine the metal type.

Fig. 6.4. Metal elements should not be removed, routinely: they can be damaged each time they are tampered with. Periodic bending of their prongs would obviously weaken them.

Removal and storage. Neither utilitarian nor ornamental metal elements should ever be removed merely for periodic cleaning. This is especially true when the metal part is attached with original early screws or nails. Left in place, these fasteners are evidence of the entire object's authenticity.

To perform some repairs on wooden artifacts, however, it *is* often necessary to remove the hardware and the nails or screws that hold it on. When that necessity arises, during conservation work, one should always consider hand-made nails and screws as individualistic parts, no two precisely alike, each slightly different from the others. To return any such item to the wrong, ill-fitting hole would diminish its holding capabilities, as well as modify the authenticity of the entire object.

When any metal part is removed from a piece of furniture, a string tag should be attached to the part, labeled with its specific location. Adhesive tape that could leave a damaging residue should not be used to identify metal pieces; and *never* attach an identification tag to a metal part with wire—that can scratch the metal.

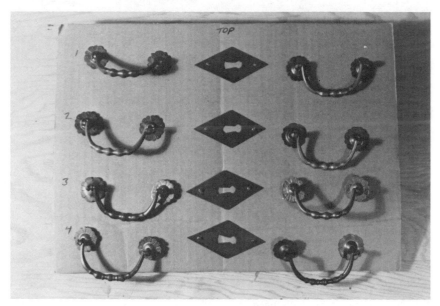

Fig. 6.5. When metallic elements are removed from a piece of furniture undergoing conservation treatment, they should be attached to a piece of cardboard for safekeeping. When the repair work is finished, all screws and nails should be put back into the furniture in the same location they were removed from.

Examine the reverse of the metal element. It may have a location number already etched in.

To be sure that ancient metal fasteners reattach the part they held to the furniture in the exact spot that they came from, draw a rough sketch of the removed metal element on a scrap piece of cardboard. Punch holes in the cardboard, showing exactly where each nail or screw came from, on the sketch; then stick each nail or screw into the cardboard sketch, following the over-all pattern of their original location (see fig. 6.5). Store the cardboard storage-template in a safe place, where the metal fasteners cannot fall out and the ornament they held cannot be scratched or dented.

Old metal fasteners—rehabilitation and reuse. Early screws and nails in wooden artifacts should not be replaced, except in extreme instances—where they have corroded to the point that they no longer function. In such instances, a conservator familiar with metals should extract them.

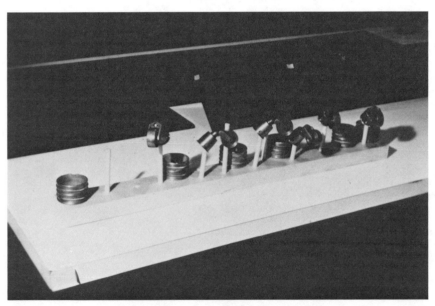

Fig. 6.6. These metal elements were removed from a piece of furniture undergoing treatment. A board with several pegs, such as this one, is useful for keeping metal elements removed from an object safely in one place, instead of rolling around loose.

After stabilization, they can be placed in a labeled jar or plastic food storage bag for safekeeping.

Nails can be extracted with the aid of a small piece of Plexiglas and side-cutters with cutting surfaces slightly ground down (see fig. 6.7).

To tighten nuts, place a piece of cloth between the nut and an adjustable wrench. Metallic elements can be scratched easily, so never use pliers or a loose-fitting wrench. Always tighten nuts very carefully, with very little leverage, because both posts and nuts can be stripped very easily.

For screws with badly worn head slots, extract the screw from its place, if that can be done, and place it in a vise between two small pieces of wood or lead, so that the screw threads won't be damaged by the jaws of the vise. Enlarge the original slot in the screw head with a hacksaw. If the screw cannot be removed, work with it in place and restore the slot with an engraving tool (see fig. 6.8). To reinsert a screw, rub beeswax on the threads to make it go in more easily. Don't use soap, because soap holds moisture. Always use a gentle pressure in tightening loose screws, and be sure that the screwdriver fits the head slot properly (see fig. 6.9).

Fig. 6.7. Extracting a nail with side-cutters. A Plexiglas strip placed beneath the cutters increases leverage and protects the finish.

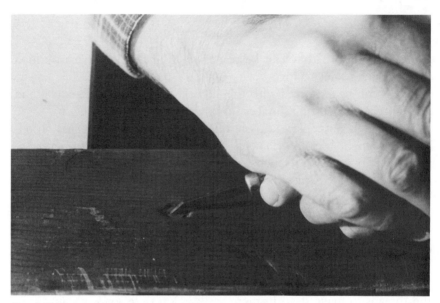

Fig. 6.8. Damaged screw slots can be reshaped with an engraving tool. Use both hands; with one hand, push in one direction and with the other, push in the opposite direction, to reduce the chances of slippage.

Fig. 6.9. Mounts should be attached with oval-head brass screws *only*—like the one shown in the center, here. Do not use flat-head or round-head screws like the ones at right and left. Always use a snug-fitting screwdriver, like the one shown. A loose-fitting screwdriver causes wear on the screw slot.

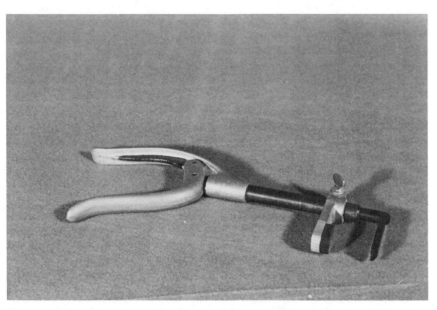

Fig. 6.10. Small nails and brads may be squeezed in with a tool like this, eliminating the shock administered by the blows of a hammer.

Nails can be tapped into place with a block of wood between nail head and hammer, or they can be squeezed in with a fitting tool (see fig. 6.10).

If the inside diameter—the threads—of the hole in the wood that a screw came from are stripped, proceed as explained in chapter 5, in the section on reattaching molding and other wooden elements by inserting a wooden plug into the worn hole that the fastener came from and inserting the fastener into the new plug.

Modern-day screws that can't be tightened—those in holes in which the threads are stripped—should be replaced by slightly larger oval-head, round-head, or flat-head screws. In working with ormolu, use only oval-head brass screws (see fig. 6.9).

Cleaning Metal Parts

Gold-plated bronze. Ormolu mounts are usually cast in bronze and then gold-plated. The classic procedure—fire-gilding—is well documented from numerous sources. Gold is an inert material and will not corrode as other metals do. It should be carefully cleaned, following these precautionary steps: Do not submerge a gilded-bronze piece in any sort of cleansing fluid; instead, remove dust and grime from it by using a soft brush to apply a solution of one part ammonia in forty to fifty parts distilled water. Follow that with a rinse application of distilled water put on with a clean brush, and dry the item with a soft cloth and an air-blower set at low heat. Never apply a polish to gilded-bronze pieces, as the gold layer is very thin and can be easily worn away.

Brass and iron. To clean brass or iron parts, place them individually—and never combine metals—in a plastic basin with warm distilled water. A soft brush can be used to dislodge dirt from the recesses. Rinse the part in clean distilled water and dry with a soft cloth. An air-blower set on warm will aid in drying the water left in recesses.

To clean recent fingerprints from brass hardware on a piece of furniture, dampen a cotton-tipped applicator with alcohol or stoddard solvent. Press out excess solvent, using a rubber glove, so that the fluid won't run on the furniture finish, and roll the applicator over the brass surface. This cleaning

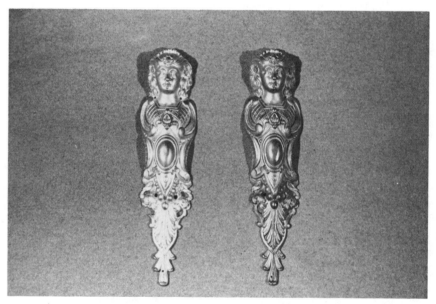

Fig. 6.11. The darker mount was subjected to visitor handling that eventually removed its original outer layer of thin gold plate.

Fig. 6.12. Clean greasy fingerprints from furniture pulls with a cotton-tipped applicator dampened with alcohol or stoddard solvent.

allows a protective brown patina to form, eventually, and removes fingerprints that will eventually etch the metal surface if left unchecked. A normal patination—browning of the surface—on brass actually forms a protective layer.

If iron hardware has a light layer of rust, soak it in kerosene for several days; then dry it with a soft cloth and allow it to dry for several days before reattaching.

Iron elements in advanced stages of corrosion—produced by damp environments—should be removed from the furniture to which they are attached and stablized. If corrosion continues, the metal will deteriorate, staining the nearby wood and finish. In such instances, carefully remove holding screws and nails, as outlined above. Brush away loose rust; then attach a string to the iron part and dip it into a metal preservative called *Ospho*. Soak the iron part in the solution for several minutes; then remove it and allow it to air-dry for at least twenty-four hours. A white precipitate may form, and that should be brushed off with a soft brush. Ospho contains phosphoric acid, so avoid skin contact. Also avoid putting painted metals in contact with Ospho, as that may make painted surfaces change in appearance. Painted metals should be treated only by a conservator.

Ospho will remove the rust from a piece of iron, and so will emulsified acids available in hardware stores. However, Ospho has the advantage of changing iron oxide to iron phosphate, thus creating a stable material. The disadvantage is that Ospho can turn the iron to a low-gloss dark gray.

Lubricating Moving Metal Parts

For lubrication of moving metal parts, such as hinges, do not apply oil and spray lubricants, because these substances can stain nearby wood and wood finishes. A tiny amount of beeswax or the paste waxes mentioned in Appendix 6 will serve as lubricants. Be sure to wipe any wax residue off the metal surface, as some staining may be possible.

The Question of Polished Metal

It is fashionable to have all metals, whether utilitarian or ornamental, highly polished. I can sympathize with the museum tour guide who is constantly asked why the collection's drawer pulls or copper pots are not as shiny as the visitors' chrome hubcaps or reproduction teakettles. Some advocates of high polish for metals argue that the original owners would have kept such objects polished, in their household environment. That may or may not be true, depending on how ambitious the owner or his servants might have been. However, with age, the finish of furniture acquires a definite patina—if it hasn't been over-restored—and old furniture probably looks a good bit different, today, from the way it looked in an early household; so why make the hardware on it incongruous to the rest of the object by polishing the metal to look new?

I hold to my no-polish policy; if, however, for some compelling reason, one *must* refurbish metal elements on furniture, the following steps should be taken:

1. Remove from the metal any old polish residue. It may be necessary to consult a conservator with a binocular microscope and the proper tools to do this as it should be done.

2. Polish the metal surface with a commercial brass polish—but

before you do, be sure to read the precautions listed among the "don'ts" below.

3. After polishing the metal element, it is important to remove all residue from the new polishing. Again, it may be wise to consult a conservator with a binocular microscope and the proper tools, to be sure that this is done as it should be done.

4. Rinse the metal object in acetone.

5. Air-dry it in a sanitary environment.

6. Apply a metal-coating lacquer designed specifically for your requirements. It is well to remember that this entire process may need to be repeated periodically, depending on the object worked on and the environment in which it is kept.

The cautionary comments that follow should produce the least damage to metal elements being refurbished:

Never use buffing wheels for quick-cleaning or applying a high polish on metal pieces, because buffing in that way will wear away the metal.

Don't use coarse steel wool; that will scratch a metal surface.

Don't use copper brighteners and dip-cleaners that contain acids.

Avoid the home recipe of vinegar and salt—vinegar is an acid, and salt—sodium chloride—can produce advanced corrosion on metals.

Commercial metal polishes of the emulsion type are not recommended, for these reasons: polish residue often lodges in recesses, causing a whitish disfigurement; commercial emulsion polishes can abrade and wear away some of the metal surface, each time they are applied; and, applied sloppily, such polishes can overflow onto the wood finish and remove some of that.

Original Components: The Voice of Experience

This is a good place for one of the best voice-of-experience stories I know. It was told to me by Rostislav Hlopoff, a retired professor from the Cooperstown (New York) Graduate Programs, and he has consented to let me publish it, just as he told it to me. The story begins—Professor Hlopoff is speaking:

It will be interesting to mention an episode of my professional life which fundamentally changed my way of thinking and working in conservation.

It was in the late 1940s or early 1950s, when the fabulous Brummer Collection moved from East Fifty-seventh Street to East Fifty-eighth Street, New York City.

One day I was working on life-size classical marble figures in the basement of the building. Suddenly, from the elevator came Joseph Brummer. After exchanging a few words of greeting, he showed me a small golden figurine one and three-quarter inches high, representing a classic divinity standing on a half-round sphere about a half-inch in diameter. He explained that this golden figurine is the finial of a Renaissance vase, off the cover, which is lost. Protruding through the bottom of the half-sphere was a sharp portion of a threaded rod which had passed through the cover. It was pinched off with a cutter. He added that he would like this sharp prong removed, in order to put the figurine, standing, in his showcase. He wrapped it again in tissue, gave it to me, and left the basement.

I returned home, later in the day, to my workshop and, with a thin file, I filed down the remnants of the rod. I then smoothed it with fine sandpaper, then on a pad with pumice, followed by rottenstone and rouge.

The same day, I went back to the gallery to work on the marble figures. Here came Mr. Brummer again, asking for the figurine. He slowly unwrapped the figure and examined my work, passing his look from the figurine to me, back and forth, several times. His look became more fiery. Then, slowly, he began to question me.

"So you filed down the prong with a fine file?"

I said yes.

"Then you sanded down the prong with sandpaper, passing to rottenstone and rouge?" His voice was becoming louder.

"Exactly, Mr. Brummer," I said.

It is interesting to note that a great connoisseur like Joseph Brummer, who in his youth worked in the studio of Auguste Rodin, was also a very fine conservator.

"I thought," he said, "that with your dental flexible shaft and a small burr, you would grind off the sharp prong and leave a scar. I would not mind to see traces of the removed screw. On the contrary; that would be the proof that it was a finial, fastened with a rod to a stone cover [the vase was of semiprecious stone]. And now what is it, I am asking you? Now it is smooth. In fact, it is not smooth, it is new! Now, if a client will ask me 'What is that? Is it a finial? How do I know?' " With each sentence his voice became louder. "Maybe it is a seal with a defaced monogram. You made a commercial job! You made it flashy, and the piece became a tricky piece, a lying piece! You removed the character of the object! Look at the difference between the newly polished surface and the gold on the rest of the object. Your work looks brassy—like a new doorknob! As I said, it is a commercial work, and the piece is ruined!" he thundered.

With this word, he left the basement. The nearby marble figures probably said to themselves, "Since the last days of Pompeii, we did not witness such a conflagration." I was petrified. After regaining my equilibrium, I walked to the exit. At the top of the landing of the first floor, Joseph Brummer was waiting for me.

Embracing me by the shoulder, he said, "Now; it is enough. Let's go, and I will show you some other objects."

I have to say that this cataclysm was a great help to me. I now understood the importance of the original surface. This scolding directed my way of thinking in a diametrically opposed way. Since the moment of the confrontation, I understood the importance of unobtrusive defects which are not disfiguring to the object. I am now applying this approach to all of my works of conservation, including furniture. My greatest work is not to overwork all of my objects.

Metal Leaf: Repairing Gilded Surfaces

Dictionaries define gilding, an art of ancient origin, as the process of applying a thin layer of real or imitation gold as a decorative element to varied types of plainer surfaces. The gold leaf used in this process is extremely thin—usually only four- to five-millionths of an inch thick— and it is applied to the surface that it is designed to ornament over a carefully prepared sandwich coat of plaster or gypsum (gesso) and glue.

Many pieces of old furniture that orginally carried gold-leaf decorations have lost part of the gilded design. Such losses are not due to accidents alone; they are usually the result of having several incompatible materials with widely differing reactions to environmental conditions trying to coexist cheek by jowl on the same surface, in the same environment. As the wooden support elements expand and contract, the hard, uppermost layers of plaster, gesso, bole, and metal leaf, less flexible than wood, change less dimensionally. That problem is inherent with furniture ornamented with gilding, and any such losses should be replaced with traditional or similar materials and techniques.

If the furniture is repaired properly and is cared for and housed in a relatively stable environment afterward, it can last for decades—perhaps centuries—longer.

Distinguishing types of gilding. The first step in repairing a gilded surface is to determine what sort of gilt surface you are working with. It will probably be one of two types, water-gilding or oil-gilding. Gold paint may also appear on the surface, depending on how much good or bad restoration has been done.

A gold-painted surface can be identified by visual inspection: it will look tarnished, exhibit a low gloss, and it will usually show brush marks. Under close examination, gold-painted surfaces appear granular. A gold "radiator-type" paint contains little or no real gold, but is primarily colored by bronze, or similar particles, suspended in a drying-oil medium. *It should be noted that traditional shell-gold, containing real gold in a water-soluble binder, does not fall into that category.* Paint with a drying-oil medium will soon tarnish, so never make any repairs with commercial "gold paint" on a gold-leaf surface. Although while fresh it might be a close match, next to a real gold surface, the paint will soon change color.

To distinguish between water-gilding and oil-gilding, take a small drop of water and place it on an inconspicuous, but representative, spot where there is no evidence of any previous repair. After several minutes, roll—don't rub—a cotton-tipped applicator over the surface covered by the drop of water. If the gold there is easily removed, the original gilding process is water-gilding; if the gold doesn't come off, the original process is oil-gilding—or water-gilding covered with an oil film.

Filling. Regardless of the original gilding process used, a careful worker, using great patience, a little practice, and reversible materials, can repair minor gilding losses.

After the process used has been determined, the damage must be examined to see whether it will be necessary to compensate for missing plaster and gesso to keep the repaired surface level. If so, dilute some commercial hide glue 50 percent with distilled water and brush the solution on the damaged area, for sizing. Let the glue dry an hour or so and then press into the area to be filled a small amount of Dap vinyl filler, a commercial product—see appendix 6. Wipe off any excess with a dampened cloth stretched over a fingertip, always wiping from the center of the fill toward the outer edge. In the same manner, after the filler has hardened, remove any excess that may have spread over neighboring areas. A dampened Q-tip is also useful for this cleaning up, especially in carved areas, but be careful not to rub the nearby original gold leaf too hard.

It is necessary to repeat the filling operation once or twice, in order to complete a good fill, because the filler may shrink slightly after it has dried for a few hours.

Inpaint the fill with the appropriate gouache color. You can use combinations of some of these colors to imitate gold: yellow ocher, raw umber, burnt umber, raw sienna, burnt sienna, lamp black, Chinese white, or new gamboge. Obviously, your repair can be noticed on close inspection, but you are only trying to make the area less noticeable and to blend in with its surroundings.

Shell gold (see Appendix 6 for suppliers) may also be used and then glazed over with one or more of the gouache colors above, to give it an aged appearance.

Metal leaf replacement. Major losses requiring metal leaf replacement should be accomplished by using materials matching the original. This work would be better left to a master gilder, a restorer, or a conservator. For the reader interested in learning background material on traditional methods, there are numerous publications. For those interested in learning more about gilding techniques, videos are also available.

It is not necessary to remove any of the remaining original gilding to replace losses and consolidate a structure. Working carefully, one can fill minor losses with materials that correspond to the original. Major consolidation may involve replacing the underlying carved wood and plaster, a job best left to a conservator or a technician who routinely deals with this type of problem.

The following steps and the accompanying photographs—figs. 6.13–6.23—document a treatment being completed. Although this treatment will not work on all similar objects, it is useful for pointing out steps and materials used by a conservator.

First, the original gilded layer was tested for solubility with a drop of water. Tests showed that this piece of furniture was oil-gilded. The surface was then vacuum-cleaned with the aid of a soft brush. Further cleaning was accomplished, after vacuuming, with a solution of 15 percent household ammonia and 85 percent distilled water. Surfaces were rinsed with distilled water and rapidly dried, taking care not to allow any of the rinse water to stand on the surface.

The next step was to brush on a solution of warm gelatine sizing, to clean away any remaining grime, to prepare the surface, and to serve as a consolidating or holding agent for the uppermost layers. It's a good idea to make up the gelatine solution only a day or two before you plan to use it, since there is the possibility of mold growth in gelatine sizing that is

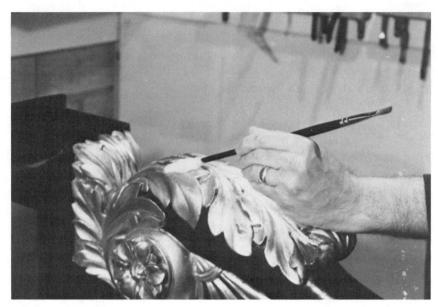

Fig. 6.13. To clean the gilded ornamentation shown here (on an artifact from the collection of the Rensselaer County [New York] Historical Society), a cotton-tipped applicator was prepared by sharpening the wooden end of an artists' paintbrush. After being dampened in a solution of 15 percent household ammonia in 85 percent distilled water, the cotton was squeezed with a rubber glove until it remained only slightly damp. The cotton was then rolled—not rubbed—over the gilded surface. As it collected dirt and grew soiled, the cotton tip was disposed of in a soft-drink can (fig. 6.15). The going-over with the ammonia-distilled water solution was followed by a careful rinse with 100 percent distilled water. The gilded surface was then dried with cotton to eliminate standing water. The soft, brush end of the paintbrush was useful for cleaning carved areas.

stored overlong. Recipes similar to the one that follows for gelatine sizing can be found in art and conservation literature, except that they include fungicides, and I hesitate to recommend their use, because of the toxicity.

The gelatine sizing needed for this process is mixed this way: Weigh an ounce of dry gelatine (see Appendix 6 for suppliers) and place it in twelve to sixteen ounces of distilled water in the top of a cool double boiler. Let the mixture stand for about fifteen to thirty minutes; then

Fig. 6.14. Do not wipe a damaged gilded surface with a cloth—instead, use a piece of cotton. If cotton snags, it won't pull off more of the already damaged structure; instead, the cotton fibers caught and held on the fragile surface will pull apart, as in the photograph, and may be gently removed without damaging the artifact further.

heat the water in the pan below. Gelatine should not be heated on direct heat, because it can be easily discolored and burned, that way. After the water in the bottom pan becomes hot, stir the solution for a minute or two. The solution can then be decanted into a clear jar, capped, and stored in a refrigerator. To use it, place the jar in warm water, and the thick gelatine will become liquid again.

After the gelatine sizing has dried, wipe off any residue with cotton balls. They are safer than a piece of cloth; if a cotton ball snags on a loosened splinter or a loose piece of remaining gold leaf, it won't pull off more of the structure—instead, the snagged fibers will pull away from the ball and remain safely held on the friable surface of the furniture until gently pulled away.

Hide glue diluted 50 percent with distilled water is brushed on over the dried gelatine sizing, and the lost gesso is replaced with Dap vinyl filler. The filled area is smoothed and any excess filler is cleaned away

Fig. 6.15. Soft-drink cans or beer cans make good depositories for used cotton waste. They are readily available: the pop-top hole is shaped just right for scraping off the used cotton; and when the can is full, it can be discarded.

with a dampened cloth stretched over a fingertip. The fill cannot be sanded, because of the danger of abrasion to the nearby original gold.

The completed fill is painted with gouache to match that originally used—in this instance, black and white gouache was mixed to match the original gray bole used.

After the inpainting has dried, a solution of acrylic resin in benzine is applied, to seal the gouache. A diluted shellac solution or a 12 percent solution of Soluvar varnish in turpentine can be substituted.

A commercial oil gold sizing is then applied and patent gold leaf laid on top of that. The repaired area should be allowed to dry overnight, and the excess gold is then wiped away with a cloth. Oil-gilding cannot be burnished, as water-gilding can.

Fig. 6.16. A warm gelatine solution to be used for sizing was prepared as in the recipe given in this chapter, in the section on *Metal Leaf Replacement.* The gelatine is brushed on the surface to be repaired, to clean away any remaining grime, impregnate the surface, and consolidate the uppermost layers. Warm the gelatine sizing by placing its container in warm water, as shown here. After the sizing dries, some residue will remain; wipe it off with dampened cotton balls.

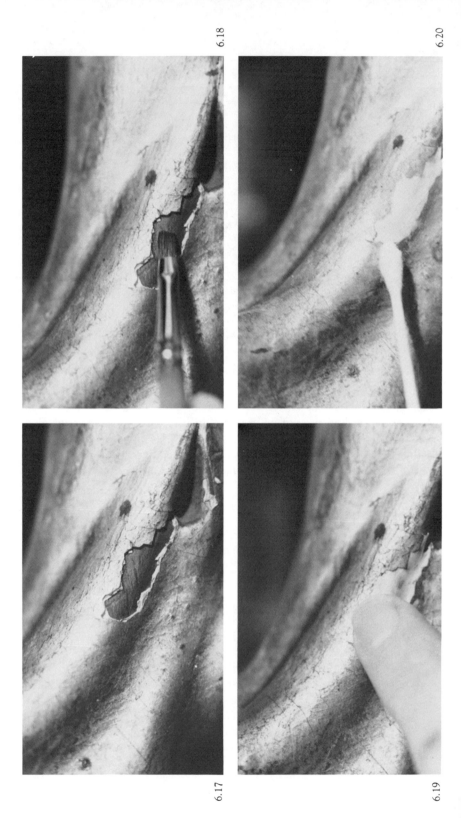

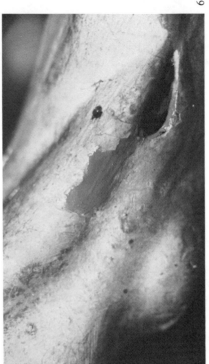

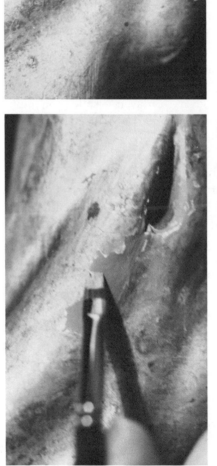

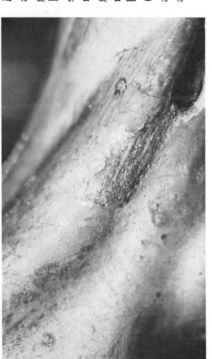

Figs. 6.17–6.23. Step-by-step replacement of minor loss of gold leaf and gesso on a gilded surface (repair site, fig. 6.17). Diluted hide glue is brushed over the area of the loss, which is then filled with Dap vinyl filler (figs. 6.18, 6.19). A smooth fill is vital; you cannot sand the area—that would abrade original gold leaf nearby. Remove excess filler (fig. 6.20) from around the fill. To match the grey bole used on this piece, black-and-white gouache was then mixed and brushed on (fig. 6.21). A solution of acrylic resin in benzine applied to size (fig. 6.22) readied the repair for leafing. (Diluted shellac or Soluvar in turpentine at 12-to-25 percent could also be used.) After new gold leaf is applied (fig. 6.23), repaired area may be "patinated" with watercolor.

৵ঈ৭ 7 ৶ঌ৵
Surface and Finish:
Care and Repair

I T might be helpful, at this point, to say some basic things about the terms *furniture surface* and *furniture finish*. These terms are interrelated and may sometimes seem to be used interchangeably, but such usage is misleading.

The *surface* of a piece of furniture is the visible, outside part of the entire structure. A furniture surface may be bare, unfinished wood, or it may include a decorative, protective layer—or layers—called the *finish*.

The original finish layer is often a transparent substance applied over a layer of stain, which has been applied to add color to the wood below. On painted furniture, one or more layers of paint form the finish, instead of a transparent layer applied over the layer of stain.

Both transparent and painted furniture finishes are often found to be made up of various layers of materials applied over the original finish of earlier years. These later additions to finishes are called "late" finishes, and, with the passage of time, "bleeding" between the layers may form a complex, homogeneous sandwich.

Since repair and maintenance of old wooden furniture surfaces involves also the finishes that cover them, both surfaces and finishes are discussed in this chapter, along with the substances most closely allied to them—fillers, waxes, and polishes.

The Furniture Surface

Accidental Disfigurement

One of the most common problems that furniture conservators must deal with is recent accidental disfigurement to furniture surfaces. Earlier

in this book, I stressed—and continue to stress—the importance, historically speaking, of retaining on old furniture surfaces the significant evidence of long usage, wear, and age; but how does one deal with the
problem of old furniture surfaces recently disfigured by accidental
scratches or dents? People who do not deal with this problem regularly,
as a matter of routine, may very well—and with only the best intentions—try to obliterate such relatively fresh blemishes entirely, abrading
or dissolving some of the wood surface and sound finish area adjacent to
the damaged spot, and what that does to the basic integrity of the piece
historically simply isn't worth the price. The experienced conservator
working with old furniture tries merely to minimize or to tone down
obviously recent accidental disfigurement.

In dealing with any such recent damage to furniture surfaces, the first
step is to examine the defaced area with a magnifying glass. If the
accidental damage is confined to the two upper layers of the surface—
finish and stain—proceed by toning down. However, if you run a finger
over the damaged area and feel a slight depression or if you see, through
the magnifying glass, that the wood itself is damaged, consider leveling
the obvious dent with a filler. (More information on fillers follows,
below.)

Repairing Minor Surface Scratches

Minor surface scratches often involve only the wax or polish layers
that cover the furniture finish. They can be repaired simply by rewaxing.
Slightly deeper scratches can be reduced—if not removed—in the same
way.

Commercial liquid scratch-remover polishes are available (see
Appendix 6 for suppliers), and they, too, serve the same purpose.
However, it is wise to confine their use very carefully to the disfigured
areas only, and not let them run over onto the surrounding area. Commercial liquid scratch-removers contain various substances, such as wood
stains, lacquer, petroleum and vegetable waxes and oils, powdered abrasives, metallic soaps, preservatives, ethyl alcohol, petroleum solvents,
organic dyes, and silicone oils.[1]

Shoe polishes with a paste base can also be used to tone down minor
surface scratches, but they, like the commercial scratch-remover
polishes, should be confined to the disfigured area only and should be
applied with extreme moderation. A single application to the scratch

itself is enough. Paste-base shoe polishes should be applied to the scratched area with a cloth or a polish-applicator brush, then buffed with a shoe brush—or a clean cloth, if the area is small. These polishes commonly contain vegetable, animal, or petroleum waxes, mineral spirits, turpentine, aniline dyestuffs, and silicone oil.[2] Be aware that some paste-base shoe polishes may contain silicone. If you discover that the one you are about to use on a furniture scratch does have silicone in it, switch to another product.

The old home remedy of rubbing over a surface scratch with a walnut kernel will tone down scratches on some finishes. It should be tried only on fresh scratches, however, because old ones may be impregnated with wax or polish that can repel this simple treatment.

Colored wax sticks (see "Fillers," below) are also useful for reducing minor abrasions. Wax sticks in a variety of colors can be made in the shop, by melting beeswax in a flat container, such as a metal jar lid. After the beeswax cools, dry pigments can be blended into it with a warm spatula. Various colors and combinations can be tried, experimentally, until the right shade is attained.

Color-matching. Whatever the method and material used in working with minor surface scratches, one should always keep in mind that exact color-matching requires considerable experience. Do not attempt to achieve perfection—simply work at reducing the abrasion and making the necessary repair as unobtrusive as possible, to preserve the finish layer of the furniture surface.

One further caution: in attempting to match colors, be careful to work under lighting conditions comparable to those where the object will remain permanently. If you work in a studio or a workshop with ordinary artificial lighting and then return the repaired piece to a room with natural light, or vice versa, the difference in color between the repair and the rest of the surface will be obvious. Lights that are color-corrected to simulate natural light can be purchased from drafting supply houses or from General Electric Company and other suppliers—see Appendix 6.

Scratches on Transparent Finishes

Inpainting and overpainting. To tone down a scratch in a transparent furniture finish, the first step is to inpaint the scratched area with a fresh mixture of shellac. In working with furniture surfaces, *inpainting* is applying a new liquid material within the boundaries of the damage. *Over-painting* is applying the new material so that it extends beyond the bound-aries of the damage. Overpainting n^t only fills in the loss, but it spreads over the surrounding, earlier finish, and—most of the time—overpainting should be avoided. Sometimes, however, disfigurements can be toned down or reduced only by glazing over with a pigment or a stain suspended in a reversible medium such as shellac.

Conditions vary with the medium used, but all repairs done by in-painting should be allowed to dry for a reasonable period of time, as the newly applied color may change considerably after drying. After freshly applied shellac has completely dried, its color may match that of the original finish. If you step back a few feet, and the scratch is difficult to see, then your inpainting was successful, and no further treatment is necessary. However, if there is an obvious discrepancy between the old and the new color, try matching the original color with gouache or watercolor. Gouache—which is, like watercolor, water soluble—tends to be opaque as it comes from the container.

To use gouache or watercolor, mix either medium with water, on an artist's palette, until you have a color as close as possible to the one needed. Apply a small amount of that in the scratched area. If the colors match, then proceed; if they don't, continue mixing the new color and try it again. It bears repeating that inpainting must always be allowed to dry thoroughly before you can be sure that the color matches successfully. In work done with either gouache or watercolor, first or faulty efforts can be removed with a cotton-tipped applicator dampened in water, if the new color is not satisfactory.

Several colors may have to be combined to get the desired effect. A darker color can be applied with a very fine paintbrush on top of the base color to inpaint the wood's "grain," pores, or rays. Grain-applicators, similar to a felt-tipped marker with a fine point, can be used. These applicators are available from Mohawk (see Appendix 6).

Wood stains. Wood stains that are alcohol-based or water-based may also be used to mend a scratched transparent finish. However, once wood stains are applied, it is more difficult to adjust their colors than it is to work with gouache or watercolor. Begin with a wood stain in a color that appears lighter than the original; let it dry; then darken it, if necessary.

Light reflections. Inpainted areas on a transparent finish may reflect light differently from the way the earlier finish did, but a top coat of shellac helps to make light reflection over a new surface repair more compatible with the older surface areas. Apply the first coat of shellac with one stroke; if you daub over the repaired area repeatedly, you may start picking up your inpainting and making a muddy mess. Allow the first shellac cover coat to dry before applying additional layers. If the shellac looks too shiny, after it dries, stroke the surface lightly with 4/0 steel wool to reduce the shine and make the repair compatible with the surrounding area.

Painted furniture. The procedure of inpainting with gouache or water-color can also be used to tone down abrasions on painted furniture surfaces. For painted furniture, however, the area to be repaired should first be primed with gelatine or commercial hide glue diluted by mixing

Fig. 7.1. Before any painted object is treated, it should be examined thoroughly by a conservator. Analysis revealed that the painted chest shown here should be given only a superficial cleaning, for these reasons: an early indigo (blue) pigment used on it had decomposed to a dark brown; an early orpiment (yellow) pigment had become almost colorless; decomposure of these pigments had caused the surface to become a dark, greenish-brown, and there was no way known today to reverse the deterioration of the early pigments and regain the original green hue still visible under the lid, where it had been protected.

Fig. 7.2. Analysis of the pigment on the surface of this painted piece indicated white lead as one of the paint elements. Photograph shows treatment of the object in progress, with the lighter half of the surface cleaned of grime.

one part glue with four parts distilled water. (See chapter 6 for preparing gelatine sizing.) Painted surfaces are complex, and the fewer new materials introduced in repairing them, the better. Repairs to painted surfaces should never be made with oil paints, which consist of pigments ground in linseed oil. The pigments and the oil change color, forming an almost irreversible film over the painted area. And don't use shellac as a top layer on painted objects; substitute, instead, a small amount of paste wax, or use Soluvar varnish.

Repairing Shallow Dents

Shallow dents in furniture surfaces can be returned to their original plane by applying heat and moisture. My experience indicates that the longer a dented surface remains distorted, the more difficult it is to correct the problem.

Hot water applied to the dented area and allowed to stand without evaporating will cause the wood fibers to swell, making them slightly flexible. To begin the hot-water approach, lay over the dented area a wad of dampened cotton the size of the dent. After a few minutes, remove the cotton and replace it with a slightly damp cloth. Put a hot iron on top of the cloth. A small tacking iron with a nonstick surface, like the one in fig. 7.7, is excellent. The heat and the moisture produce steam that eventually returns the swelled wood fibers to their original plane. If the dent remains after this treatment, see "Fillers," below. Although a fill may make a surface repair obvious, filling may be less disfiguring than simply leaving the dent.

This heat-and-moisture treatment to correct shallow dents in furniture surfaces usually damages the surrounding finish, and that must then be corrected by inpainting and reapplication of a new finish over the damaged area.

Whitening of Finishes

Water condensation from a cup, glass, or vase that comes into contact with a furniture finish can cause rings, spots, or other disfiguring areas of whitish, translucent discoloration (a bloom). One recommended solution for that is to apply a paste wax over the discolored area and rub it until the white disappears. For information on waxes, see below.

If treatment with wax is not successful and if the discoloration is confined to a small area only, another solution is an old home remedy that is relatively safe, if used with care and moderation: mix a small amount of mineral oil with the ash from a cigar or a cigarette, to form a paste. Rub this paste on the whitish area with your fingertip for a short time; then dry the spot with a soft rag.

If that does not work, try mixing a little mineral oil with rottenstone. The mild abrasions that take place when this mixture is rubbed on the whitened area may reduce the blemish. Again, don't try to achieve perfection; be satisfied if the treatment simply tones down the disfigurement. If you go too far, you could abrade more of the finish than is necessary.

A similar disfigurement extending over larger areas can result from a humid environment, and this frequently happens to the finish of furniture stored in damp basements. Evidence of such moisture damage first appears as a discoloration that is dark-bluish in color. These blemishes serve as a warning that the environment is not satisfactory and that a dehumidifier should be used to reduce the amount of moisture present. If unchecked, these areas of moisture disfigurement usually soon turn whitish, spreading over the surface and becoming difficult to remove.

Fillers

Serious dents, depressions, and losses greater than the size of small screw heads in a furniture surface can be considered major disruptions. They are usually filled with material duplicating the original as closely as possible.

Losses *smaller* than the size of screw heads in furniture surfaces can frequently be traced to repairs or recent damage. Following is some comment on commercial products, as well as fillers made in the laboratory or shop, for dealing with small losses.

Dowels to fill holes. If, during a former repair, screws or nails were used to attach an unnecessary fastener to a piece of furniture (see fig. 7.3), such a fastener should be removed. This necessitates filling the holes that the screws or nails made in the wood. If such holes do not occur in a joint of the furniture—as in the sofa in figure 7.4—some of the void can be filled with an undersized dowel smaller than the hole, secured with hide glue and putty (see below). A dowel that fits too tightly could eventually result in the wood's checking or splitting. If the hole involves a joint, it could mean that a reconstruction of the area might need to be made by a cabinetmaker or a furniture conservator. Don't rely on a joint repair with just a new, snug-fitting dowel, as that remedy will probably become loose over a period of time.[3]

When you use a dowel to fill a hole, drive the dowel in a quarter of an inch or more below the surface, to provide space for a tapered plug (see fig. 7.5). These plugs can be purchased ready to use (see list of suppliers, Appendix 6), or they can be made with cutters available from the same supplier. Obviously, tapered plugs can even be used if no dowel is pressed in below as a foundation for them. However, make sure that the plugs are of the same type of wood as the original wood, and that the grain of the plug is oriented in the same direction as that of the original. Press such plugs into place and cement them in with hide glue.

The sort of cutters needed for this work should provide considerable versatility. For example, holes sometimes need to be plugged at varied

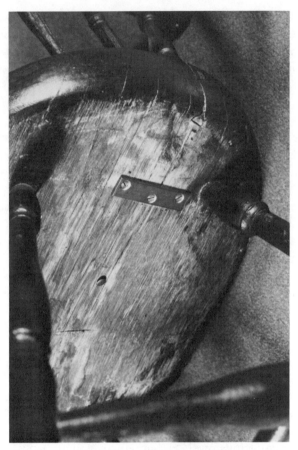

Fig. 7.3. A close look at the underside of this wooden chair seat illustrates the way mending plates often cause additional damage as the structure of the wood they are attached to fluctuates.

angles, in varied kinds of cuts—transverse, tangential, or radial. The same kind of wood should be found and marked in an area that shows a similar figure. With the plug cutters, the plug can be cut out, stained, finished, and pressed into the hole, resulting in a nearly invisible repair.

Dough-type fillers and sawdust. Commercial dough-type fillers can be purchased to fill small voids. Such fillers commonly contain some of these ingredients: textile spirits, alcohol, nitrocellulose, resin, vegetable

Fig. 7.4. These L-brackets were attached at various places to the stretchers and legs of an early sofa. Only about 25 percent of the brackets were used to hold joints together; the rest were attached as a "precaution." All of these brackets were added during an early restoration, unnecessarily causing irreparable damage.

oil, wood flour, calcium sulfate, aliphatic keytones, magnesium silicate, toluene, plasticizers, and dyes.[4]

Filling material can also be made by mixing sawdust with hide glue or with an aliphatic-resin glue. The consistency of this mixture can be varied, as needed.

Commercial and homemade fillers. Neither commercial nor homemade fillers will be a close match for the wood being repaired, and if they are used at all, they should be confined to very small losses. In addition to being obvious in appearance, they may become brittle, resulting in cracks around the perimeter of the place filled in. They have been known to fall out when the wood expands and contracts around them.

Some are more useful than others. All of the commercial fillers should remain in place longer if the hole being mended is first coated with hide glue or an aliphatic-resin adhesive. The filler material is

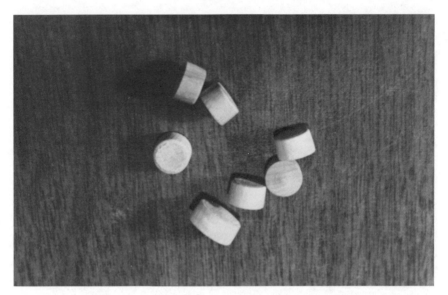

Fig. 7.5. Tapered plugs like the ones shown here can be used to fill large round holes left in wooden structures when screws are removed.

Fig. 7.6. Losses at various places on this piece of furniture had been replaced at some time with plaster. Plaster, of couse, is inflexible and makes a brittle fill. As the wood expanded and contracted around the brittle fills, the plaster broke up and fell out, leaving gaps.

pressed in with a finger, spatula, or putty knife, and leveled off. It may shrink upon drying, necessitating an additional application.

Also, if you use a commercial filler, don't bother getting a colored one, as most of the time colored commercial fillers will not match your wood. Instead, purchase a neutral, light-brown filler and then inpaint.

If the wood surface to be repaired is painted, a different type of filler is required: *Dap vinyl* is what is needed to fill losses in a painted surface. Make sure you use *only* the Dap product marked *vinyl*, as several types are available from the same company. Dap vinyl will remain flexible, and it is reversible with water. A hard, brittle filler, on the other hand, may eventually fall out. Dap vinyl can be inpainted to match the surrounding color, so it can be considered even for repairing unpainted surfaces.

Various colors of commercial wax sticks are also recommended as fillers. They can be heated and mixed to provide a wide range of colors. Good, workable wax sticks can also be prepared in the workshop, by melting and mixing together carnauba and microcrystalline waxes, fifty-fifty by weight. (See "Waxes and Polishes," below.) The appropriate dry pigments are then stirred in.

Hard colored-wax sticks may be softened with a small spatula warmed over an alcohol burner. The softened material is then carved away from the wax stick and pressed into the surface loss; or it may be dripped in. The wax filler contracts after cooling, so a second application is usually

Fig. 7.7. Colored wax sticks, heated with a tacking iron, are excellent filler material.

necessary. The cooled fill is leveled off by rubbing with a cloth stretched over a fingertip.

Wax fills follow the conservation philosophy of being easy to remove by carving out and cleaning off residue with turpentine or benzine. In small holes, a colored wax fill can be almost invisible. In large holes, the presence of monocolored, smooth wax fill is more obvious, and, during dry periods, when the surrounding wood contracts, cracks can develop around the perimeter of such a fill. However, the advantages of wax fillers far outweigh their disadvantages, so I recommend their use.

All of the above materials will also work for deep abrasions or accidental losses and defacement in wood. However, keep in mind that larger disfigurements should be filled with wood whenever possible.

NOT *recommended: stick shellac.* Do not use stick shellac as a filler, for these reasons: It does not imitate the appearance of finished or unfinished wood in any way; it is brittle and can easily crack and fall out of the area it was used to fill; if it does fall out, what remains of it in the damaged area may be difficult to remove; and it often damages the original adjoining finish around the defacement.

The Furniture Finish

For centuries, finishes of varied kinds have been applied to the surface of wooden furniture to give the bare wood protection and to provide some decoration. Varnish, shellac, lacquer, paint, gesso, and metal leaf are among the many kinds of materials that have been used as wood finishes, through the years.

Some finishing materials form a seal over the surface of the wood and provide a base for polish. Transparent finishes, such as clear varnish, shellac, or lacquer, give uniformity to a wooden surface and lend depth and intensity to its appearance. Wax, which has been used as both a finish and a polish, was commonly relied on as a finish by cabinetmakers in colonial America. Other finishing materials frequently mentioned in colonial account books and probably applied as finishes are resins and copal varnish. These components were used in various proportions, along with other ingredients in numerous formulas for finishing materials.[5]

The surface of most historic furniture existing today will not have retained its original finish—or, at least, the original finish will probably

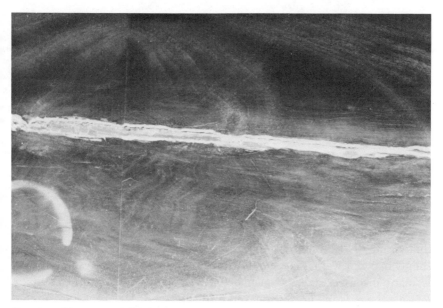

Fig. 7.8. The type of fill shown here (on an artifact from the collection of the National Park Service's Martin Van Buren National Historic Site) is rarely successful and often induces further damage in its removal. The white water-ring visible at left is an additional incidental defacement.

Fig. 7.9. Early stick-shellac repairs such as these are often disfiguring.

not be visible on the surface: it, or most parts of it, will most likely have been covered over by more recent finishes and thus, in addition to being hidden from view, the original finish has probably been saturated by successive layers of polishes, stains, or additional finishes put on top of it, over the years.

Removing Flawed Finishes

With the passing of time, the original true color and beauty of the natural wood in an old piece of furniture is gradually obscured under a darkened finish; and it sometimes happens that an owner may not find that result of the natural aging process appealing. Also, some owners simply may not want a piece of furniture on which the finish shows flaws. In many instances, when that happens, the solution has been to strip or remove the existing finish from old furniture.

The question of stripping finishes. Stripping, it may be argued, irretrievably destroys some of the historical integrity of a piece of furniture. No serious collector, dealer, curator, or conservator would recommend stripping historic furniture. An old piece of furniture that has been stripped loses much of its significance as a historic artifact—and much of its value as a source for future research. Stripping may also reduce the actual, hard-cash market value of the object. Furniture—and furniture finishes—will, if properly cared for, last for generations. Many furniture conservators maintain that no one has a right to destroy any part of a historic artifact simply for arbitrary reasons.

One valid exception to that belief may be made if the need should arise to remove a late nineteenth-century or a twentieth-century finish that has been improperly applied over an older or perhaps an original finish. Disfigurement frequently results when old furniture refinished in the 1800s and early 1900s was not sufficiently cleaned before a new finish of varnish, shellac, or lacquer was applied. When that sort of thing happened, the newly applied finish, without a properly strong bond, gradually became brittle, flaked off, and, with time, gave the furniture surface a crackled appearance.

A strong case could also be made for removing a finish badly disfigured by fire or accidental water damage.

Other exceptional instances that might justify removal of the finish occur when a linseed oil finish has been applied recently, or when a piece of furniture has one or more layers of recently applied paint.

Fig. 7.10. This small table (shown under raking light in fig. 3.5) had complex finish problems. Analysis indicated that it had an original eighteenth-century finish that needed to be stabilized. That type of complex treatment should be undertaken only in a conservation laboratory, as too much original material could be lost without a thorough understanding of the entire structure.

When expert help is needed. In all instances, removing the top finish is a job for the professional, who can control the materials used and the methods of application and prevent any possibility of the work's damaging the underlying finishes. It is not necessary to clean off everything down to the bare wood. Working in a laboratory, the conservator can determine the specific type of finish—or finishes—present, and usually has the required skills and experience to remove recent finishes of shellac, lacquer, and paint and still retain lower, older layers of earlier oil finishes. If the recent finish is an oil type, the problem of removal without harming earlier layers is difficult. Any decision about what method to use in removing a flawed finish requires, first, a complete examination of each individual piece of furniture; removal of the top finish then should be carried out by a conservator.

And painted surfaces are so complex that only a professional conservator should treat them—no one without proper training and experience should attempt such work. In dealing with painted objects, the experienced conservator knows how to remove one layer of paint at a time. There are no shortcuts for treating painted objects, and one should regard with extreme caution anyone who claims that there are. What may work for one painted object may damage another. Without a thorough understanding of the physical and chemical properties of each individual paint layer on the artifact, it is possible to cause irreversible damage. The painted object may have only a single layer of paint, or it may have a finish consisting of many layers—each one a complex structure containing color particles suspended in a binder. When fresh, each layer was both plastic and elastic; but over the years, paint layers lose those properties. The result is embrittlement and cracking.

Some guides to furniture care recommend using oil paints for inpainting or overpainting losses on painted furniture, as well as for scratches on other finished surfaces. *Under no circumstances should any paint with linseed oil be used on any historic object.* Linseed oil paint is irreversible; as it ages, the oil becomes darker, and the paint pigments frequently turn darker or lighter. Gouache or acrylic paints are suitable substitutes, if it is necessary to inpaint abraded portions of a painted finish. Acrylics soluble in petroleum solvents are suggested (see glossary). The pigments in gouache and acrylic paints also change color; but with them, there isn't the problem of having the medium also turn darker. Also, gouache and those acrylics soluble in petroleum solvents are much easier to remove, if the need for removal arises.

Routine preliminaries. An untrained individual can make preliminary tests to gain a general idea of the type of finish present, always remembering to apply the testing substance to the top finish in a small, inconspicuous area. Tests to determine types of finishes should be made with

Fig. 7.11. Half the darker top layer of the finish has been removed from this painted clock face, photographed undergoing treatment. At top, near the arch of the dial, it is evident that large areas of the original painted flowers were removed in an earlier restoration.

Figs. 7.12 and *7.13.* This chest-on-chest has been subjected to restoration abuses. At some time in the past, damaged areas were painted over with an oil-based paint. Close-up at right shows how, with time, the oil-based paint darkened markedly over the damaged area.

cotton-tipped applicators and solvents. The applicator should be dampened with benzine or turpentine and rubbed over a very small test area on the furniture finish. That test rub is followed by a light going-over with a clean cotton applicator, to pick up and clear away loosened grime and the remaining solvent. That procedure will remove most wax residues from the test spot.

The next step is to test for the presence of shellac in the finish. Another cotton swab should be dampened with alcohol and gently rubbed over the test area that has had the wax removed. If the finish in the test area reacts to the alcohol by becoming sticky, that is a fairly certain indication that that finish is shellac. If the surface remains hard, the next step is to use a fresh cotton swab to test the spot with lacquer thinner. A softening of the finish and some stickiness at this point suggest the presence of lacquer; if the surface remains hard, however, then a drying oil finish of some type is present.

Before doing anything about removing a dark or grimy finish, try some of the tests recommended in the chapter on cleaning. Results of such tests are often surprising, and working with the information they provide can sometimes help to preserve an early finish with its patina.

Patina—and its raison d'etre. We should say something here about *patina.* Patina is *not* disfiguring dirt. It has been called "a glow or aura which emanates from an object." [6] The patina on a piece of furniture represents part of the history of the individual object, resulting, as it does, from the cumulative appearance of the various finish layers as each has reacted to the environment.

Patina begins when the original finish oxidizes. During that process, the finish allows light to pass through to the wood below. Reacting to the light, the wood changes its appearance, too, just as the oxidizing finish does, though perhaps more subtly. These combined changes of finish and wooden surface over a period of years can produce *furniture-finish patina.* Much old furniture, as time has passed, has had successive layer on layer of wax or other finishes applied over the original coat. Eventually, some areas of these accumulated finishes may have been rubbed off, but whatever remained also changed in appearance—or in the way light was reflected from the finished surface—and all of that contributed to the patina visible on the finished surface.

Another type of furniture patina results from frequent handling during the object's use. That kind of patina is particularly visible on surfaces such as unfinished table tops or wooden drawer or door pulls, both of which are subject to the repeated touch of many hands when the object functions in a living or working environment. This sort of "contact patina" is not to be confused with the ordinary grime that accumulates from much custodial or visitor handling.

Also, moving parts of such objects as spinning wheels are often darkened by the oil occasionally used on them as a lubricant. Such stains are evidence of use and are a form of patina.

Refinishing

Various options for dealing with the finish on each individual piece of furniture should be considered. For example, it may be possible to apply a new finish to certain parts of a piece of furniture, instead of refinishing the piece entirely. Consultation with a furniture conservator is recommended—a conservator can be helpful in selecting the best option. If a conservator is not available, however, and if the decision is made definitely to refinish the piece, then it may be possible to obtain help from a local cabinetmaker.

Cabinetmakers commonly achieve perfection in their work. Unfortunately, a "shiny-perfect," new-looking finish is out of place for museum objects that really should reflect the patina of their true age. A melding of the cabinetmaker's "brand-new" approach with the conservator's philosophy of never overworking a piece would be a good course to follow. (Overworking a finish comes from use of strong abrasives, bleaches, and strippers.) A look at some other furniture that has been carefully refinished without sacrifice to its aged appearance could help as illustrations in talking with a cabinetmaker about refinishing.

Recommended Finishes

Three reversible and recommended finishes are wax, shellac, and lacquer. Wax, about which there is much to be said, is discussed further in the section on "Waxes and Polishes," below.

Both shellac and lacquer are solvent-release types of finishes—that is, a solid film is formed after they are applied to a wooden surface and their thinner or solvent evaporates. Both shellac and lacquer can be softened again by reintroducing the correct solvent or thinner (reversible).

Shellac. Shellac is a solution made of alcohol and the resinous secretion of the scale insect *Tachardia lacca*, or lac. The insects feed on the sap of certain tropical trees, and their resinous secretions—also called lac—harden on exposure to air. After crude lac is gathered from a tree, it is crushed. The largest particles, called seed lac, are selected for making the best grade of shellac. The lac is heated, squeezed through a cotton bag, and worked into a plastic mass. It is then stretched into thin sheets. The sheets are slowly cooled and broken into flakelike pieces. Shellac comes almost entirely from India, although it is also produced in small quantities in other areas in Southeast Asia.[7]

The patina of a furniture finish may be saved by building up several layers of shellac or lacquer before using an abrasive—very fine steel wool, or sandpaper—to smooth the surface.

Both shellac and lacquer can be applied and modified to achieve almost any desired appearance. They can be glossy or flat or anything in between, according to their application by an experienced cabinetmaker.

Fig. 7.14. Water damage is evident on the finish of this table.

Fig. 7.15. After proper treatment cleared up the water damage visible on the table in fig. 7.14, the wood of the repaired table was given a new shellac finish.

Shellac is a capricious substance, especially sensitive to moisture during application. It should be applied in an environment as close to 50 percent relative humidity as possible. I once had the unfortunate experience of applying several layers of shellac when the humidity was above 70 percent. The result was that the surface didn't dry properly. I had a deadline to meet, but no environmentally controlled finishing room was available. I had to remove all my shellac work and replace it with lacquer.

Shellac is available commercially in dry flakes or as a liquid preparation. Both forms come in orange or white. Orange shellac can be used to produce an appropriate warm tone. For use on furniture, shellac should be purchased in dry form only and mixed with denatured alcohol in a glass jar. Purchased in liquid form, its shelf-life is limited; and buying it in an undated container is an open invitation to major problems. I do not recommend any commercially prepared shellac more than a few months old, as the result of its use may be a finish that won't harden. If you do buy shellac in liquid form, I should recommend using it as soon as it's purchased; and before using it on *furniture,* test it on a scrap piece of wood. If it remains sticky on the test piece and does not dry properly, return it for a refund.

Liquid shellac is priced according to what is called its *pound cut:* one pound of dry shellac flakes dissolved in one gallon of alcohol will yield a *one-pound cut;* two pounds of dry shellac flakes in one gallon of alcohol will yield a *two-pound cut.* The two-pound cut is a useful preparation and may be thinned with more alcohol if needed. The price goes up as the pound cut increases.

Unless you need more than a gallon, I suggest smaller proportionate amounts, such as eight ounces of flakes in one quart of alcohol. Mix the dry flakes—either white or orange—with the alcohol (denatured) in a glass jar. Allow the flakes to dissolve in the alcohol overnight. Shake the jar and stir the mixture occasionally. After the flakes have dissolved, strain the fluid through fine cheesecloth. The solution may look cloudy, but it will dry clear or translucent. Do not save shellac left over from a project for very long—throw it out after ten to twelve weeks.

Lacquer. Lacquer, like shellac, is a solvent-release type of finish. Coatings made from synthetic resins and cellulose derivatives are commonly known in the trade as lacquers—usually clear.[8]

Lacquer can be applied in very thin coats, which is excellent for use on furniture. It has the unique quality of attaining extreme hardness. It provides considerable protection and can be highly polished.[9]

"Feeding" a Furniture Finish

Never use the much-publicized recipes for "feeding" a furniture finish. *Feeding* is a term that was at one time used fairly freely in the trade. It will make you feel as if you are keeping your furniture as happy as your household pet, and for that reason the expression is now commonly used by people who are trying to sell a product. It is very much to the point to remember that wood and wood finishes do not have digestive systems, however. (Another misconception about wood is that it "breathes.")

The "feeding" formulas found in some books on furniture restoration often advise use of drying oils, such as linseed oil. Variations may contain nondrying oils. A nondrying oil has the undesirable characteristic of doing just what the name implies—not drying. The unfortunate result is a sticky, dust-attracting surface. Nondrying oil may, in addition, actually trap any solvent with which it is used and thus soften an earlier finish below the present one.

A widely recommended formula containing turpentine, vinegar, and linseed oil must be used judiciously. To put it more directly, once every several years may be too often to use it, because of the eventual damage that its overuse can cause. I know of at least one major American collection that has been harmed from the extensive application of this formula. If you do use it, be sure to wipe off most traces of it with a clean cloth, immediately after its application.

Types of Finishes To Avoid

Avoid finishes that contain a drying oil (linseed oil is one example). Such finishes can be classified as reactive finishes,[10] which change chemically upon application. Through oxidation—the absorption of oxygen—they polymerize, or form a tough, hard film on the surface. As time goes on, that film becomes more difficult to soften. Other materials that should be avoided include those that follow.

Linseed oil. Linseed oil was a widely used finish in the past, because it was easy to acquire, easy to apply, and easy to repair. Those attributes do not imply that it should be used today, even over an earlier finish of the same type.

Linseed oil is obtained from the seeds of flax, and it is available commercially as either *boiled linseed oil* or *raw linseed oil*. Raw linseed oil contains an element called *foots*.[11] Foots are parts of the oil that will never harden; during the refining process, they are removed, like dregs, from the raw linseed oil by refrigeration and filtering. One cannot produce *boiled* linseed oil simply by boiling the raw version.

If linseed oil is applied periodically on a piece of furniture, a sticky, dust-catching, grime-holding surface develops. The furniture surface will blacken, as the linseed oil turns progressively darker on exposure to air and daylight and as accumulating dirt sticks to it. Moreover, boiled linseed oil polymerizes—or changes composition—as it dries, forming a tough, hard surface. Any attempt to remove the so-called impregnated "feeding" mixture will involve the use of solvents so strong that their use will inevitably destroy much of the original finish.

Varnish. Varnish is a nebulous term that one dictionary defines as "a preparation made of resinous substances dissolved in an oil or in a liquid like alcohol which evaporates quickly (spirit varnish) and is used to give a glossy surface to wood."[12]

Modern varnish is a reactive finish comprised of synthetic alkyd resins and linseed or soya oils combined under pressure and heat, with driers and thinners added.

It has been suggested that the origin of the generic term *varnish* is based on the story of Queen Berenice of Cyrene, whose golden or amber-colored hair was accepted by Venus as an offering for the safe return of Queen Berenice's husband. Or the name may have come the Latin *veronice* and Greek *berenike*, which referred to a sandarac resin exported from the ancient city of Berenice in Cyrenaica, now eastern Libya, bordering on the Mediterranean Sea.[13]

Tung oil. Tung oil, also called Chinese wood oil, is obtained from the seeds of *Aleurites cordata*, *Aleurites montana*, and *Aleurites fordii*, grown in China and surrounding countries. A similar oil is produced in Florida and Japan. Tung oil dries more quickly than linseed oil. If applied in heavy coats, it can wrinkle. It produces a dull finish, yellows considerably. *Never* let your hands come in contact with it during application or clean-up; it may cause diseases of the skin.[14]

Ester-gum or resin-modified alkyd varnish. Ester-gum or resin-modified alkyd varnish is commonly used on flooring, to withstand wear. This very hard varnish is of course not suitable for use on historic furniture. Alkyd resins are obtained from polyhydic alcohols and are frequently combined, industrially, with cellulose nitrate.

Phenolic-resin varnish. Phenolic-resin varnish is also made from a synthetic resin that will dry harder, tougher, and with more moisture-resistance than alkyd varnish. It is primarily used for exterior use, because of its flexible properties, and it is commonly called *spar varnish.*

Polyurethane varnish. The term *polyurethane*—and other product names containing *poly-* as an element—is used to refer to a number of various polymers, plastic-like substances used chiefly in making various materials, among them adhesives and resins for coatings. The usual version of polyurethane varnish sold commercially will be modified with alkyd resin or drying oil.

Caveat

Commercial preparations often have names designed to make the product more appealing. Who could resist buying a "Scandinavian rubbing oil that will impart a suntan-like glow to your furniture"? The contest continues, between the advertiser's wiles and the wariness of the potential buyer. Always read product labels and, if you are considering refinishing furniture, avoid formulas that contain the materials in the paragraphs immediately preceding this one. On the other hand, if the product is to be applied to something other than a historic piece of furniture or an artifact, many of the preceding substances are appropriate.

Waxes and Polishes

Wax has been used as a finish for wooden furniture for centuries. Unfortunately, it has also been abused as both finish and polish nearly as often as it has been used. Today, it appears as a protective coating on an earlier finish more often than it serves as the finish itself. In view of its long history—and excellent service—as a finish for wooden surfaces, however, I should suggest that, if you must consider applying a new finish over an original one, try wax, instead of the routinely used alternates, varnish, shellac, or lacquer.

Applying Wax

The method used in applying any of the various wax preparations discussed below can determine each product's effectiveness. If these waxes are applied over earlier layers of polish, the result can be a sticky surface that attracts finger marks and dust. Any wax build-up that has accumulated on a finish should therefore be removed before a new layer of wax of any kind is put on.

A shoe polish applicator brush can be used to put a coat of wax on carvings or moldings. A shoe polish brush will also work in applying wax on a flat surface, but for flat surfaces toweling is better. In waxing a flat surface, rub the wax in a circular motion and finish with strokes in the direction of the wood grain. It is most important not to load the applicator (either brush or cloth) too heavily; only a small amount of wax, about the size of a pea, is sufficient for an area measuring two to three square feet. After the wax has been put on, wait several hours for the thinner or turpentine in it to evaporate before buffing the surface with a soft, clean

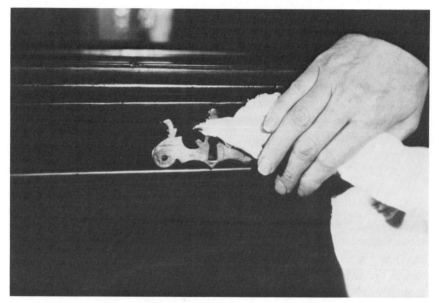

Fig. 7.16. In routine polishing or dusting, great care must be taken not to let cleaning cloths snag any part of a piece of furniture or any of its attachments.

cloth; otherwise, less shine is produced, and your buffing doesn't do much but move the wax around on the surface.

Available Products, Pro and Con

Various kinds of wax preparations on the market today include paste waxes, liquids, and aerosols. Paste waxes are more difficult to apply than the liquids and aerosols, but their properties are more in harmony with conservation philosophies and practices than are the others. Any liquid or aerosol product that claims to polish, wax, and clean, all at the same time, should be avoided. Serious deterrents to use of such claimants are the possibilities inherent in them for damaging furniture finishes: some of the chemicals used to liquify such products can, after several applications, attack finishes or make a surface tacky; and as liquid and aerosol wax products age, some of their ingredients may permanently saturate a finish; and they may change color, which also affects the color of the finish.

Paste wax should never be applied to furniture that has an oil finish less than one or two years old, however, because the wax may soften such a finish. And never apply paste wax to bare wood, because dirt may be forced into the wood, along with the wax, and, once the wax is applied, the ground-in dirt is difficult to remove. An exception to this caveat is the bare wood of drawer runners: paste wax can be used there to lubricate the runners, ease sliding, and reduce wear. Paste wax should never be applied over a *dirty* finish, either, although it can be used to remove superficial dirt if it is applied with a light hand and if the applicator cloth is rotated frequently.

If the object being worked on has recently had a wax build-up removed, it is wise to repeat the wax application and buffing. The second application helps to achieve a uniform layer of the wax finish.

Types of Paste Waxes

Beeswax. Commercial paste waxes are a combination of different waxes, each with various properties. One widely used component in commercial paste waxes is beeswax, produced by the common bee, *Apis mellifera.* Beeswax—primarily melissyl palmitate ($C_{15}H_{31}COOC_{30}H_6$) —

is the secretion of organs on the underside of the working bee. Bees use it to form the cells of the hive's honeycomb. Beeswax is obtained by melting the honeycomb, removing the impurities, and retrieving the wax.

Beeswax can be purchased as either yellow or white cakes, the white kind having been bleached of its natural yellow color. Bleached beeswax is more brittle than the unbleached yellow, especially when it is cold; and white beeswax may remain noticeably white in the crevices of an artifact to which it is applied. If applied improperly and used alone, beeswax can remain soft and collect grime and finger marks. Both the white and the yellow beeswax can be modified as needed, however, by the addition of dry pigments.

To make a good beeswax furniture polish, follow this recipe:

• Shred a cake of wax with a carving knife until there are enough wax shavings to fill a jar approximately two-thirds full.

• Pour in turpentine (either pure gum spirits of turpentine, oil of turpentine, wood turpentine, or distilled turpentine) until the jar is three-fourths full; then cover with a lid. A piece of plastic food wrap should be used to cover the underside of the lid so that the turpentine will not soften the lid liner and its adhesive.

• Place the jar in a warm area for a few days and rotate or stir the contents several times a day. The polish-making process can be accelerated by placing the jar of wax and turpentine in warm water, to apply mild heat to the contents. The soft, light paste wax that will form, after a few days' time, can be used to polish light-colored surfaces.

• To darken a wax polish made in that way, stir in a small quantity of dry-pigment lamp black or burnt umber. If you desire a selection of colors, varying amounts of pigment can be added to the wax base.

Microcrystalline waxes. Microcrystalline waxes are plastic materials derived from petroleum refining. In addition to higher melting points and viscosities than paraffin waxes, they include a wide range of physical properties, varying from soft to hard. *Cosmolloid 80H* is a microcrystalline wax that can provide a harder material than beeswax. A recipe that I have used successfully is this one:

• Place 20 grams of Cosmolloid wax in a jar. Melt the wax by heating the jar in a double boiler. Cosmolloid wax is hard, and it may take nearly an hour to melt it over boiling water, so check frequently to be sure that the water hasn't all evaporated. The heater used must be electric or another flameless type.

• When most of the wax has liquified, pour fifty milliliters of odorless paint thinner into a second jar—one that is large enough to hold both the thinner and the melted wax. Work in a well-ventilated room and be sure that none of the paint thinner comes close to the heater. Warm the paint thinner in the double boiler also. Turpentine or ordinary paint thinner can be used, instead of the odorless thinner. However, the odorless kind has advantages if applied in a household or in a place frequented by visitors, since its smell is less disturbing.

• After the thinner has warmed, quickly pour the wax into it, forming a homogenous mixture. Stir, if necessary. Cap the jar and let the mixture cool, but store it in a warm place.

Beeswax-Cosmolloid combination. A third form of furniture wax can be made by combining beeswax and Cosmolloid, one part of each in two parts of odorless thinner or turpentine. Combining both the hard Cosmolloid and the softer beeswax produces a material that dries hard, yet is easier to apply than the regular Cosmolloid preparation. Manufacturers sometimes change components, or phase out a material. If and when Cosmolloid is not available, other microcrystalline waxes may prove to be an acceptable alternative. To date, I have not experimented with other similar waxes.

After applying any of the above three formulas, wait several hours before buffing.

Renaissance Wax. Renaissance Wax is a good commercial wax recommended for functional pieces used regularly. It contains only Cosmolloid wax, a polythene wax called BASF Wax A, and white spirit. I apply Renaissance Wax about every six months to my kitchen table, at home. Before applying it, I wipe off any previous layers of wax with toweling dampened in odorless paint thinner, then dry the surface with a clean cloth.

Renaissance Wax functions well, just as it comes from the container, on small objects; applied to large areas, however, it often streaks and is difficult to buff. To prevent that problem, dampen the waxing cloth with a small amount of some liquid thinner such as paint thinner, turpentine, or benzine. Always be careful to avoid rubbing hard enough to cause additional damage to objects with loose joints.

Put a small amount of Renaissance Wax on a soft but strong cloth, such as a cotton bed sheet or a diaper. Rub the wax on with a circular motion, but finish with strokes along the grain of the wood. Let the solvent evaporate for fifteen to twenty minutes—a waiting period of several hours is not necessary with this wax—then buff the surface with a soft, clean cloth in the direction of the wood grain.

Paste waxes that perform well, if properly applied, in addition to Renaissance Wax, are Butcher's White Diamond Wax; Behlen's Blue Label Polishing Paste Wax (in natural, light oak, or brown); and Staples Paste Wax (in light or dark brown).

Several other commercial paste wax products perform satisfactorily, providing protection and a polish. Most are easily applied and can be conveniently removed. Apply them according to manufacturers' directions on the containers they come in, but use all of them with restraint, applying only once every three to four years.

Commercial waxes often contain varying proportions of the following ingredients:

Carnauba wax: Carnauba wax is a hard yellow wax from the leaf of a Brazilian palm tree, on which it forms as a deposit. The palm leaves are cut and dried, and the wax powder is scraped off and melted.

Candelilla: Candelilla has a lower melting point than carnauba, but has similar characteristics. It is obtained from the stem of the leafless Mexican plant *Pedilanthus pavinia.* Candelilla is often used as a replacement for carnauba, as it is cheaper to purchase.[15]

Paraffin wax: Paraffin is a distillate from petroleum and sale. Commercial paraffin is a whitish, translucent material and it comes in various melting ranges, all quite low. It may be slightly more expensive than candelilla wax.

Ozokerite wax: Ozokerite wax is obtained by mining. Its hardness ranges from soft to hard.

Additional common ingredients of paste waxes and their proportions follow: mineral spirits, zero to 80 percent; emulsifier, 3 to 15 percent; water, 10 to 80 percent; and preservative, .1 to .5 percent.[16]

Paste waxes may also contain traces of shellac, perfume, pine oil, dye, alkyl sodium sulfate, soaps, bentonite, ethylene glycol, glycerine, gum tragacanth, gelatine, gum arabic, hydroxyethyl cellulose, isoctyl phenyl polyethoxy ethanol, petroleum synthetic waxes, quarternary ammonium compounds, silicones (generally less than aerosol types, which can contain up to 4 percent), synthetic resin, and turpentine.

Although the list of ingredients that can be found in paste waxes is long, it can be considered only a reference point. Most commercial waxes contain few of these compounds in trace amounts, and little or no damage would result from conservative application.

Compare the products available to you, however, and avoid those containing the highest percentages of any ingredient (including water), with the exception of waxes and solvents.

Polishes and Polishing

The idea that furniture must be polished frequently, perhaps once every two weeks, is ridiculous. Frequent polishing is a pitch that advertisers use, to promote the sale of their products.

It should not be necessary to apply a wax polish to furniture in a museum environment more frequently than every three or four years, except for objects that are frequently handled. These pieces may have to have a wax layer removed and reapplied two or three times a year.

When polishing or dusting, watch out for loose pieces of veneer, molding, or furniture hardware that may be pulled loose, bent, or broken by the action of your cloth. It is, of course, preferable to make certain that such elements are firmly attached before polishing. Do not polish any surface on which there is flaking paint, gesso, or metal leaf. Conditions such as that will continue to deteriorate, and the piece on which they are found should be treated as soon as possible. Metal leaf surfaces should not be polished, anyway, and unless specifically recommended by a conservator, neither should painted surfaces.

⤙ 8 ⤚

Good Housekeeping for Artifacts

JUST as an improperly maintained atmospheric environment can be ruinous to furniture collections, so poor housekeeping can contribute toward that. Haphazard housekeeping routines for either the artifacts in a collection or the place where they are kept invite insects and rodents and serious problems. Dusting and running a vacuum cleaner at least once a week in normal traffic areas are essential procedures. Cleaning routines for areas where there is heavy traffic will vary, depending on visitation volume and weather conditions; two or three times a week, however, is good practice. Storage areas, even though they are visited only occasionally, should also be maintained on a regular schedule.

Dust

A fair rule of thumb is: If you can see dust, throughout either building or collection, you should clean more frequently.

Allowed to accumulate, surface dust can seriously damage the surface of a piece of furniture by trapping moisture there during periods of high humidity. A dust build-up can also cause damage by abrasion.

To remove dust from furniture, wipe the furniture surface gently with a soft, clean cloth. A diaper, fragments from an old flannel garment, or nontreated commercial bulk dust cloths may be used (see Appendix 6). Rotate the dust cloth frequently. After you wipe over two or three average-sized pieces of furniture, go outside the building and shake the accumulated dust out of the cloth. Several cloths mean fewer trips to the door. The cloths should be machine-washed after they become moderately soiled—that will be about once or twice a month, in a well-maintained small museum or average-sized household.

Feather dusters are not recommended to dust with, because they may snag or tear off peeling pieces of inlay or veneer or other components. As an alternative to feather dusters, use the safer 100% lambs wool dusters. They are available at hardware stores; or, see List of Suppliers.

Also not recommended are commercial aerosol "dust attractors" or "dust magnets" that can be applied to the dust cloth. They should be used only in moderation, if at all. If too much solution is applied to the dust cloth, the aerosol deposits an oily residue that holds dust on finished surfaces and makes its use self-defeating. It won't create a wax build-up, but it *will* create an *oil* build-up, and you don't want that on your furniture either.

To apply a light coating of commercial aerosol to your dust cloth, spray a fine mist for a second or two on a clean cloth. Do this outdoors, so that the airborne droplets of nondrying oil do not settle on nearby artifacts, textiles, and paintings. Never reapply spray to the same cloth until after the cloth has been washed.

Never use a so-called tack-cloth for routine dusting. Tack-cloths are used in cabinet-making shops for wiping sawdust off surfaces before finishing. As the name implies, tack-cloths are treated cloths that feel sticky or gummy. They should not be used for dusting finished pieces because all they do is attract and absorb abrasive dust particles and move them around on the surface—almost like a very fine sandpaper.

Small decorative objects placed on top of pieces of furniture may need to be moved while you are dusting. Be sure that there is a clean, safe place nearby to set them down. Dust only one piece of furniture at a time, so that you won't assemble a large collection of artifacts in one spot, inviting an accident. Slippery glass and glazed ceramic pieces should be lifted with bare hands only; natural oils and acids from bare hands cannot penetrate these glassy surfaces, and you can grip them more securely without gloves. Small items of *unglazed* ceramics, metal, stone, leather, paper, or textiles, however, *do* have porous surfaces that *can* be damaged by skin secretions, so they should never be picked up with bare hands—they should be handled only with clean white cotton gloves. (However, see chapter 9, on wearing gloves to move furniture.) These white gloves should be machine-washed, as dust cloths should be, but the gloves will need washing even more frequently than the dust-cloths.

A protective layer of cork can be placed under abrasive objects. Cork sheets used for gasket-making can be purchased from hardware or auto supply stores. Set the artifact on the cork sheet; trace on the cork the outline of the object's base; then cut out the cork shape and place it under the artifact. It is not necessary to glue the cork mat to the bottom of the artifact. There have been instances where glue not completely dry harmed some types of finishes.

There are also small, self-adhering cork disks that can be purchased, ready to be placed on the underside of an object. (See Appendix 6.)

Never use felt as a buffer for small artifacts to sit on: felt is hygroscopic and can trap moisture on a finish.

Detached Veneer and Inlay Fragments

In dusting the collection, be careful not to snag loose pieces of veneer or inlay. If you have a cleaning staff, encourage them to report any such loose pieces that they know of and ask them to report any accidents with these materials immediately.

Good-sized pieces of veneer or inlay that have pulled loose and become separated from their original base should be lightly identified *on the reverse side, with a soft pencil.* Never attach tape as a label on finished veneer surfaces; if necessary, you can attach a label to the reverse side. Torn-off pieces of veneer or inlay should be stored in a box or a drawer, cushioned with packing material or bubble-wrap. Smaller bits and pieces can be kept in a labeled plastic bag or a vial. Large or small, such loose bits should be kept in a safe place, preferably within some part of the same object from which they came, such as a drawer. And all separated elements, partial or complete, should be reattached as soon as possible. See chapter 5 for information on this kind of repair work, or get in touch with a conservator who may be able to spend some time doing remedial on-site reattachment. It is well to keep in mind that, if you have a large collection, you may have quite a bit of this kind of damage, and your accumulation of detached pieces and similar crumbs can fairly quickly grow to fill several shoe boxes. At some places, these shoe-box collections have expanded to fill crates—and even rooms. In many instances, unfortunately, most of the detached pieces will never be replaced, as labels identifying them were not made at the time the damage occurred.

Cleaning Marble, Leather, and Fabric

Marble components, such as tops, should be cleaned routinely only with a vacuum cleaner. Special techniques for the kind of additional cleaning required for badly soiled marble or for ivory piano keys appear in chapter 4.

Fig. 8.1. Fortunately, many of the decorative elements that became separated from this piece of furniture were collected and saved by professional staff members.

Vacuum cleaning only is also recommended for writing surfaces made of fabric or leather. For more rigorous cleaning of these surfaces also, see chapter 4. Use the screen-wire guard discussed there in going over these substances with a vacuum, to eliminate pulling up the fabric or leather edges.

Apply no excessive moisture to fabric or leather surfaces, because they are probably held down with water-soluble adhesive, and they may also shrink.

Spilled Liquids on Furniture Finishes

Overfilling flower vases is a common cause of damaged furniture finishes everywhere. If you do inadvertently overfill a flower vase placed atop a piece of valued furniture, remove the vase immediately, along with the coaster or anything else on which the container may have been resting. Blot up the water with anything absorbent that is readily available—a clean, soft cloth is preferable, but a handkerchief or a handful of paper tissues will do, as speed is essential: if water is left on the finished furniture surface, a bloom will appear, and the piece will be disfigured. After you've wiped away the spilled water, allow ample time for everything to dry.

Immediate action is also essential if any alcoholic drink is tipped over or spilled on a piece of furniture. Alcohol, of course, is a solvent for shellac, which is often a component in many furniture finishes. It may liven up a dull party if the only available blotter for an alcohol spill on your furniture is your shirt or blouse. Never hesitate—use it! Unless you blot up alcohol quickly—and be very careful just to *blot; don't rub*—you will have a disfigurement on the artifact's surface the size and shape of the alcohol spill.

Your Cleaning Staff

Make sure that the people who clean your building are aware of the need to use cleaning equipment carefully, because furniture finishes can be destroyed by repeated contact with wet mop strands or abrasive broom bristles, and furniture feet, legs, and aprons can be bumped, dented, scratched, scarred, and disfigured by carelessly wielded broom handles and vacuum cleaner wands. The wet mop strands mentioned are not hypothetical—I've seen a maintenance person industriously flopping a dripping mop smack up against a medieval chest. The marble floor being mopped in this vigorous way about two or three times a week was commendably clean; but the feet on the medieval chest were clean, too— absolutely stripped of any patina, finish, or paint.

The reader who is either a curator, a collector, a homemaker, or a conscientious cleaning person takes pride in the artifacts that make up each individual collection. Some of the material written here about cleaning is obvious to such people—they already know how to make their own cleaning system work best for them. There is, however, a small percentage of people, sometimes found in large cleaning staffs, who try to accomplish the admittedly mundane work of cleaning as rapidly as possible, with little concern for collection pieces. It should therefore be the standard responsibility of anyone who supervises a cleaning staff to do the following:

1. Provide proper cleaning instructions through demonstrations. Workshops by conservators are very helpful.

2. Discuss with the cleaning staff the responsibilities each should undertake. Make each staff member aware of the historic significance of collection pieces. Ask them to report at once any damage they see or any damage caused accidentally.

3. Point out especially vulnerable objects—loose legs, peeling veneer, flaking paint, and so on—and bring the list up to date at staff meetings.

4. Provide the cleaning staff with proper cleaning materials and equipment and provide an easy system for replenishing expendables. Nothing is more frustrating than beginning a job and finding that you are out of supplies.

5. Provide the cleaning staff with the proper safety equipment. (See chapter 11.)

❧ 9 ☙
Moving and Storing
Furniture and Artifacts

A S anyone who has shifted furniture from one place to another will tell you—at the drop of a crate—there are certain ways to go about it that make the work go more smoothly. Many good procedures can be acquired on the job, as experience accumulates; but if you begin by observing the general principles that follow, your furniture-moving can be done more safely, more easily, and with appreciably less damage to both staff and stock than might otherwise be.

Preliminaries

Before lifting a piece of furniture, workers should remove from their persons and their clothing all items of apparel or ornament that might scratch or snag the furniture. That includes rings, watches, lockets, key chains, belt buckles, pens protruding from pockets, and similar things.

To move chests, desks, or any other piece of furniture containing drawers, the first step is to take out the drawers. Using chalk or small self-sticking labels, mark correct placement for them on the underside and reinstall them after the piece has been moved to its new location. Lock cabinet doors so that they won't swing open while the piece is being moved. To secure doors that don't lock, tie a string around the entire object. Remove all loose finials; if there are a great many, tag them for proper identification and put them into a safe, padded place, to be reattached after the objects they adorn have been moved.

Before moving any artifact, especially a large piece of furniture, make sure that the route it must be taken over is free of clutter and that the place where it is to be set down is clear.

Figs. 9.1 and 9.2. Never lift a chair by its back, as shown at left. The correct way to do it is shown at right: bend your knees to support the weight of the chair and use both hands to lift it by the sides of the seat.

Lifting and Shifting

Anything larger than a small side chair should be moved by at least two people. If no helper is available when you are ready to move the piece, wait; never push a piece of furniture across the floor to get it from one place to another.

Before lifting any heavy object, make sure that whatever you and your partner are going to grasp to move the piece by is firmly attached to the rest of the structural framework.

As you begin lifting an object, *don't bend; squat,* instead, keeping your back straight. The back doesn't have to be absolutely as vertically straight as a plumb line—it should just be straight. Be sure your body weight is centered over your feet. Lift by straightening your legs and keep the load close to your body. To unload—again, *squat;* and, again, keep your back straight. If you have to turn with the load, avoid any twisting motion—instead, shift your feet. If you must lift something heavy above waist level, don't try to do it in one motion: instead, set the load down on a table and change your grip before lifting it higher.

To lift a chair, grasp it by the sides of the seat.

A four-wheeled cart is excellent for moving heavy objects around inside a building or to a loading dock. Pad the cart with movers' blankets to absorb shocks. You will need a considerable quantity of padded blankets. They should be purchased locally. Inspect them before buying, to be sure that they contain a sufficient amount of padding material and that they are well stitched.

Marble tops. Marble tops *can* be transported on a cart, but if you do plan to move them that way, be certain that they are well padded—even the slightest vibrational shock may crack a slab of marble. Such pieces should always be well supported, and *they should be moved vertically.* If marble slabs are carried by hand, they should be carried as sheets of glass are carried: vertically, never horizontally.

Sometimes, after a marble top has been removed, you may notice that it does not rest squarely on top of its case. Do not add shims or wedges under the marble to correct that. Shims placed directly under one side of the marble may cause it to crack if anything heavy, such as a large

Fig. 9.3. Marble tops should be transported and carried vertically, as glass is carried, to prevent the type of breakage shown here.

candelabrum, is placed on top of it. Instead of shims, place a wedge under the leg or the foot of the base piece, below the gap between case and marble top. That usually will force the case to conform to the flat plane of the marble top.

Leather tops. Do not transport heavy leather-topped pieces upside down. That can damage fragile leather. Move such pieces on their backs—or, better, have a furniture conservator remove the leather top. The rest of the structure can travel upside down.

What To Wear

Forget about wearing white cotton gloves when moving furniture: cotton gloves will reduce your grip and may even cause your hand to slip on a polished surface. Cotton gloves may even stick to a finish. A few years ago, I thought that white gloves should be used for lifting any collection piece. One day I started to lift a piece that had a slightly sticky finish, caused by high relative humidity. After I had lifted it, one of my gloves stuck to the finish, and my hand nearly slipped out of the glove before I recovered my grip with the other hand.

A few years ago, I was at a workshop-seminar on furniture analysis. All the other speakers were wearing white gloves as we moved several pieces of furniture in front of the audience. Rather than mention my opinions—and problems—with gloves, I let the matter go and put on a pair of them. As a colleague and I turned over a small drop-leaf table with a high-gloss finish, I felt my cotton gloves lose their grip and begin to slide on the finish. Fortunately, I was able to recover my grip, just in time to avoid an embarrassing disaster.

Do not wear gloves when handling glazed ceramics or glass, for the same reasons that you don't wear them to move furniture: they can cause you to lose your grip on the object being moved.

Do, however, wear gloves when handling textiles, stone, unglazed ceramics, metals, paper, and leather. Acid, salt, grime and oils can be transferred from bare hands to these objects, and clean gloves will help prevent that.

Short-Distance Moving

If pieces of furniture are to travel in a vehicle—a van such as the one shown in fig. 9.4 is excellent for this purpose—movers' blankets should

Fig. 9.4. A vehicle such as this van, owned by the state of New York, is excellent for transporting furniture.

Fig. 9.5. Although any vehicle used to transport furniture can be outfitted with tie-down devices, it is safer, in moving small loads of furniture, simply to place the pieces carefully, in loading, and use a great many movers' blankets to pad and hold them in place.

Fig. 9.6. Eyes and cleats can be permanently attached inside a vehicle to be used in transporting furniture. These devices are useful for tying down pieces of furniture when the van is full, to keep the load from shifting.

Fig. 9.7. The break visible here occurred when a table was improperly packed for moving.

first be laid on the floor. Case pieces should travel only on their backs: that position not only reduces vibrations, but also reduces the chances of the piece's falling over, in case the vehicle makes a sudden stop or is involved in an accident. Roll several blankets together to serve as bolsters between the inside walls of the van and around the sides, top, and bottom of each piece of furniture.

If several pieces are being moved at the same time, fit the smaller ones in around the larger pieces, with blankets for protection between them. Always stop and check the load after the first mile or two, to see how it is settling.

Use plenty of blankets and tie the artifacts down only if necessary. If they must be tied, use nylon rope about a half-inch in diameter and pad the area where the rope touches the object. The transport van should be outfitted with numerous cleats and eyes to anchor tie ropes (see fig. 9.5).

Never stack artifacts one atop another, unless such crowding is unavoidable. In such instances, place the lightest pieces on top.

Artifacts and Thermal Shock

Always consider the possibility of damage from thermal shock to fragile objects being moved. I once heard of an individual who brought a rare and valuable glass object to a curator for examination during winter weather. When they walked out to the car after the examination, bringing the glass artifact from a warm room into sub-zero weather, the object shattered.

In transporting artifacts locally, during the winter, therefore, always cover them with a few blankets, even if you will be traveling only a short distance. Wrap each object before taking it out of a heated building and make sure that the interior of the transport vehicle has already been warmed before the wrapped artifact is brought outside to load into it. At destination, leave the blankets over the artifact for at least an hour or two after unloading—preferably, overnight—to allow the object to make gradual adjustment to the new environment without undergoing thermal shock.

When transporting artifacts during the summer, park the van in the shade, so that it will not be prohibitively warmer than the interior of the air-conditioned building that the artifact came from or will be taken into.

Long-Distance Moving

Always be aware that objects being shipped over long distances can undergo thermal shock if introduced to extreme temperature variations in different parts of the country. If an object is packed in ninety-degree heat in Los Angeles, for instance, and then is air-shipped to Chicago, where it may sit for two days on a loading dock in temperatures of zero to a few degrees above that, damage can certainly result.

Fiberglass house insulation in a packing crate provides excellent protection against temperature changes in shipping.

Shipping Crates and Packing Materials

To transport furniture over short distances within the local area, it is unnecessary to construct shipping crates. For short moves, they only add to the over-all weight of the load, and they are time-consuming to make. However, if you need to ship something for a long distance, a proper crate and suitable packing material are worth the time and trouble it takes to assemble them. Figures 9.8–9.17 outline the construction of a shipping crate from start to finish.

I once worked on a rocking chair, shipped inside a well-made crate by a commercial mover. The chair had broken into smithereens. The problem was in the packing material—crumpled-up newspapers. Newspapers make good packing material, but this packer had used far too many—so many, in fact, that they provided no cushioning effect whatever, and pressure applied to the outside of the crate was transferred directly onto the paper-packed rocking chair.

Bubble-wrap, styrofoam pellets, and sheet foam available from a packing-goods supplier or manufacturer, make excellent packing materials.

Storage Space and Surroundings

The size of your collection determines the number of rooms that should be set aside for storage. Establish a systematic arrangement for storing your collection; set aside an area for furniture; glass should be separate from metals, and so on. Store framed objects, including mirrors, paintings, empty frames, and so on, on movable screens or in properly constructed storage bins.[1]

9.8

9.

9.10

9.

9.12

9.

9.14

9.

9.16

9.

Fig. 9.8. Points to observe in constructing a shipping crate for an individual piece of furniture begin here and continue through fig. 9.17. The illustrations were photographed as a crate was being prepared for the chair shown here being measured for fit against two sides of the crate. Even after careful measuring beforehand, it is always safer to take two sides of the crate, before they are fixed together permanently, and place them around the object to be sure they are going to be the right size. Any modifications needed will be obvious in the early stages of construction.

Fig. 9.9. Crates for shipping furniture should be held together with waterproof plastic resin glue, in case they are exposed to rain; and the glued sides of the structure should be reinforced with screws, not nails. Nails could work loose inside the crate, during shipment, abrading the object held within. Screws also make the entire structure more stable and easier and safer to dismantle in uncrating the furniture.

Fig. 9.10. The sides of the crate are clamped together while the glue hardens. Again, the chair to be shipped is placed inside, to double-check dimensions.

Fig. 9.11. Detail of "keepers" built into the shipping crate: the padded, rectangular keeper in the bottom of the case will prevent the chair's shifting from side to side; and a padded auxiliary board fits into U-shaped blocks (upper right) in the crate's sides, riding over the chair's stretcher and keeping the chair from moving up or down. *Note: One of the biggest mistakes packers can make is adding superfluous packing material. I saw one chair that was surrounded so tightly by packing material that pressure applied to the outside of the shipping crate was transferred straight through the packing material, breaking the chair apart.*

Fig. 9.12. Two lengths of ribbon—front-to-back and side-to-side—hold the seat cushion in place during shipping.

Fig. 9.13. The top of this shipping crate has weatherstripping attached, to seal out dust and moisture.

Fig. 9.14. Proper stenciling of instructions on the outside of the crate is crucial.

Fig. 9.15. The receiver should be given clear directions about the best way to unpack without damaging the crate and its contents.

Fig. 9.16. The shipping crate should also carry clear instructions for repacking it for the return trip. The arrows on the lid must be lined up in co-ordination with those on the side.

Fig. 9.17. The finished crate, loaded and ready for shipping.

Fig. 9.18. A portable forklift is useful for moving heavy objects.

Try to arrange for storage rooms that will permit efficient movement of the collection in and out, in the event of an emergency. For heavy objects, avoid designating a storage room that can be reached only by going up or down narrow stairs.

Storage rooms should be free of leaky ceilings and, if possible, free of any overhead water pipes and heating ducts that may develop leaks.

Do not store flammables near the storage area. If possible, keep such substances in a separate building, away from all collections.

Storage room windows and doors should be well-secured with locks.

Install insulation around doors and windows to reduce the entry of airborne dirt. Cover windows with painted plywood or thick black fabric, to prevent light from leaking in. The black fabric should be lined with a white fabric that faces outside, to reflect sunlight and heat away.

The storage room environment should, of course, be controlled. There should be some air circulation and low artificial light levels (see chapter 2).

Placement of objects within the storage area. Plan available storage space carefully. Utilize wall space to put up hanging racks for swords, rifles, and frames. Install shelving made from three-quarter-inch plywood and two-by-fours or slotted-angle hardware. Never make shelves out of particle board, as some grades of particle board may decompose. I've seen old particle board buckle under a load and the screws holding it pull out from the framework.

Apply polyurethane to shelves, and never overload them. Place small, shorter pieces of the collection toward the front, where they can

Fig. 9.19. Metal-slotted angle is excellent material to use as a framework for shelf construction. Shelving made of three-quarter-inch plywood coated with polyurethane is held in place with screws.

Fig. 9.20. On shelves of metal-slotted angle and plywood, objects are easy to locate and the space provided prevents their being stacked on top of one
another.

easily be seen, instead of placing them near the back, behind bigger,
taller artifacts.

Collect broken-off fragments or pieces separated from the place
where they were originally affixed—such as veneer segments—and put
them in labeled containers; store them in a specific area, where they can
be easily found for reattachment; or store them inside the objects from

which they originally came, making a note in the records telling where they can be found.

Place carpet on the floor beneath fragile objects to protect them, in case they're dropped. Do not use rubber-backed carpet that can decompose, producing sulfur fumes.

Maintenance Checklist for Storage Rooms

Below is a checklist for periodic maintenance of a storage room; but before you concentrate on the checklist, make sure that the room is completely clean and well organized.

1. Periodically, check the relative humidity and the temperature of the storage room with a psychrometer, hygrometer, or hygrothermograph.

2. Schedule daily maintenance for humidifiers and dehumidifiers, to be sure that the relative humidity is kept between 40 percent and 60 percent.

3. Keep the area clean to discourage insects and rodents. Run a vacuum cleaner throughout and dust the collection monthly.

4. Do not block aisles or use them as catch-alls. Clutter makes cleaning harder and impedes the movement of objects in an emergency.

5. Do not store objects near heaters or heating ducts.

6. Never stack other objects on top of furniture.

7. Use furniture for storage only if the piece is in good condition and if the objects stored are light-weight (see below).

8. Do not cover objects with plastic sheets that trap moisture; instead, cover with bed-sheets.

9. Do not use aerosol insect repellents on collections of artifacts: tiny droplets of the spray may settle on objects and damage them. Use insect repellent strips, instead, and hang them near the ceiling, because they function better at higher temperatures. Replace the strips every four months.

10. Periodically, check the plumbing if the storage room has pipes running through it.

Obviously, collection pieces should not be used as functional pieces in exhibit areas or in the offices of an institution. If storage space is at a minimum, case pieces can be used for storage—of light-weight items only—so long as drawer bottoms are in good condition and drawers are not opened and closed frequently. To reduce friction and wear each time the drawer is opened, apply a light coating of paste wax to drawer runners. Line drawers with a neutral or nonacidic paper; nonacidic *Glassine* is useful. To prevent further wear, avoid daily opening and closing of drawers and doors.

❧ 10 ❧
Insects and Other Pests:
Some Things To Do about Them

A
MONG the other hazards that can damage furniture are the flying, creeping, crawling, clawing, and chewing kind that are a constant threat—insect and small animal pests. Of them all—rats, mice, bats, pigeons, and a pantheon of insects—the insects may be the most plentiful—and the most troublesome. They are usually small—sometimes minute—and difficult to detect; and through sheer numbers and a formidable persistence, they have been gaining on us since the time of the pharaohs. Following are some effective ways to protect your furniture collection from them.

Detection

The first clue to the presence of wood-boring insects in a piece of furniture is often a small amount of what looks like fine sawdust, underneath an object. This is *frass,* and part of it is fine sawdust, mixed with the leavings of the wood-borers at work chewing on your artifact. You may notice such traces beneath a newly acquired piece of furniture, or under something you've had for years. Small amounts of frass may go unnoticed by even the best of housekeepers, especially if the object that has been invaded is on a carpet. If the floors are uncarpeted, make a routine "flashlight test" once every few months: turn on a flashlight and sweep the beam across the floor to create a raking light, against which the wood-borers' telltale residue can be more readily seen. Areas where you need to clean better will be embarrassingly obvious—but what you need to look carefully for are clusters of light-colored, fine, talc-like particles.

149

Fig. 10.1. In this example, insect infestation was thought to be confined to this small element of one piece of furniture. The drop-turning was removed from the piece and fumigated, but it was soon evident that the whole object was infested, necessitating total fumigation.

Fig. 10.2. This is a good example of evidence revealing an active wood-borer at work.

If you see any, look at the wood of the piece of furniture directly above them, to see whether any small holes appear there. *Dark* holes indicate that, although borers have been there, they are presently inactive at that spot. But if you see *light-colored* holes that contrast sharply with the solid wood, you have current infestation. These light-colored holes are called *bright holes* (see fig. 10.3). You may even see particles of frass being pushed out of a hole or two, as the insects work.

If you are uncertain about the presence of insects during a first investigation, but suspect that they are there, move the piece of furniture under observation to an area isolated from people and from the rest of the collection—perhaps to the garage or the barn. Make certain that the

Fig. 10.3. Detail of a musket stock covered with holes made by a wood-boring insect. The "bright holes"— the light-colored ones—indicate insects currently active.

object is placed away from people, where nobody can accidentally bump against it; if it is bumped in the right spot, old frass material can be dislodged, and you would be getting misleading information from that faulty evidence. Set the furniture on a big piece of dark-colored paper and leave it there for a few days. If you see little scatterings of frass under the object when you return to check it, then you have wood-borers.

Combating Wood-Borers

Wood-borers can enter your collection or your household in various ways: in a recently acquired piece of furniture, in a load of firewood, on clothing, or through open doorways or windows. Other types of insects and pests, as well as wood-borers, can also enter in those ways. Some worthwhile precautions to take include these:

1. Before acquiring a new piece of furniture, inspect it for "bright holes," which mean that active borers are currently present and at work.

2. Install window screens throughout the building that is to house your furniture.

3. During warm seasons, when insect activity increases, do not store firewood inside the building that houses your collection.

4. Maintain a clean environment. Insect activity is encouraged by such poor housekeeping practices as tiny food particles left lying about and by hair trapped in carpeting or in the cracks between boards in a bare floor.

The general name *powder-post beetle*—or powder-post borer—is applied to any of several types of beetles whose larvae feed in wood, reducing the interior to powder. Three distinct families of this pest are the *Anobidae*, which includes the furniture beetle and the deathwatch beetle; the *Bostrychidae*, or false powder-post beetle; and the *Lyctidae*, or true powder-post beetle.

The *Lyctidae* variety commonly damage furniture in North America. Their average length is about an eighth of an inch. They appear flat, with a distinct head. Adult powder-post beetles lay their eggs in tiny cracks and openings in wood surfaces. When the eggs hatch, the larvae burrow deeper into the wood. As they bore through the structure, they weaken it by creating long, hollow passageways.

Powder-post beetles cannot digest cellulose, but they can digest the starch content of the wood. Eventually, when they become adults, they eat their way to the surface and leave the tunnel-weakened wood structure through emergence holes, flying off to continue the family tradition. These flight holes can be numerous, peppering the surface of the wood with holes about one-sixteenth to one thirty-second of an inch in diameter.

Fumigation chambers. Insects harmful to collections can be destroyed by professional techniques in fumigation chambers. This treatment subjects the infested object to a toxic gas, commonly a gas with a small percentage of ethylene oxide. The treatment is one of the most effective. It is extremely hazardous to use, however, and must be applied only in a suitable chamber, by trained operators. Residual traces of the insecticide can remain present in some materials for weeks, even months, so that a period of isolation after treatment is necessary. The use of ethylene oxide is now under strict federal and state regulations. Much has recently been learned about ethylene oxide and alternative methods. The reader is advised to consult the references in the bibliography and to keep abreast of current literature.

The isolation method. One method you can follow to eliminate wood-borer infestation that is confined to only one or two objects is this: first, place the pieces to be treated in an isolated room. Do not choose a room that contains a freezer or a refrigerator. Vapors from insecticides—including mothballs—can filter into freezers and refrigerators, even when their sealed doors are closed, to contaminate and impart a foul taste to stored food. Purchase from a local supplier plastic bags manufactured for enclosing mattresses and other large objects during shipment. It may take several phone calls to locate such oversize bags, but most cities have at least one supplier. Objects that will not fit into the largest bags obtainable can be covered completely with a painters' polyethylene drop cloth, with all edges sealed to the floor with duct tape. For small objects, use a plastic garbage bag or a leaf-disposal bag. It is always better to reinforce the enclosure by using two bags or two drop cloths; the double thickness of the covering reduces insecticide-odor migration.

Hang a no-pest strip inside the bag with the infested object, making certain that the strip does not come in contact with the enclosed piece of furniture. Hang the strip close to the surface of the bag, from an auxiliary support. Seal the bag with a twist tie, duct tape, or weights. If the treatment area is in a cool place, put an exposed light bulb outside the bag, near where the no-pest strip is hung, but far enough away so that heat from the bulb won't melt the bag. The purpose of the bulb is to elevate the strip's temperature slightly, since the insecticide in the strip functions better at temperatures above 65 degrees Fahrenheit or so.

One unfortunate feature of this home remedy is that the furniture being treated must remain in its mini-environment for at least a year. Because of the life cycle of the infesting insects, the treatment may not affect all stages—adults, larvae, and eggs—and, if the furniture is left in the treatment bag for a shorter period, some insects would simply fly out to lay more eggs, perhaps within your collection.

In addition to that, the no-pest strip must be replaced every four months, because its effectiveness diminishes after that length of time.

Other pesticides. Other insecticides can be introduced to supplement the isolation treatment; used only by themselves, however, other products may not be very effective.

Take a liquid ant poison or a roach product and fill a syringe with it. If these products are not available in liquid form, then spray the contents of an aerosol can of the insecticide into a jar and fill the syringe with the liquid from the jar. Systematically inject the insecticide into each hole in the infested furniture, taking care to wipe from the surface any liquid that runs out. Unfortunately, this method may produce few or no results, because the liquid insecticide should come in actual contact with the wood-borers to do its work.

Another method of treatment, perhaps more effective, is to place a large quantity of mothballs in the treatment bag. For this purpose, purchase only mothballs in containers that list peradichlorobenzene as an ingredient; those listing naphthalene are less effective.[1]

Mothballs, like the no-pest strips, are volatile, and when they are used in large amounts, they may damage certain finishes.[2]

It is well to keep in mind that pesticides of any type, including mothballs, can be dangerous to humans. Never use any pesticide when children are in the vicinity, since children have little resistance to its effects. Adults working with these substances should always wear good respirators and polyethylene gloves and work where there is good ventilation.

Presently some institutions are utilizing careful and precise freezing techniques to eliminate insect activity. (For more information, see Florian's "The Freezing Process—Effects on Insects and Artifact Materials," listed in the bibliography.) Although the process is deadly for insects, it is safe for humans. Unfortunately, most pieces of furniture are too large to fit in a freezer.

Also, there are problems with the process of freezing metals, painted arti-facts and objects composed of several different materials, as are most furni-ture pieces.

Other Insect Pests

The wood-borers described here are only one of many kinds of insects that can damage furniture and other wooden artifacts. Other destructive insect pests are silverfish, clothes moths, flies, termites, carpet beetles, cockroaches, carpenter ants, and cigarette beetles. These insects are only general types that have various family members, some causing more damage than others. Each should be dealt with in specific ways.

Flies and spiders need this additional comment: they leave behind acidic bits of excrement—the familiar flyspeck effect—that can damage furniture finishes, paintings, and many other surfaces. Infestations of both flies and spiders can be reduced by the use of no-pest strips. Hung in an attic window, where these two types of pests seem to congregate, a no-pest strip soon demonstrates its effectiveness. Please refer to chapter 11, on safety practices, before using the strips.

Professional Help in Exterminating Pests

If your collection infestation problems go beyond one or two pieces of furniture—or one or two unwanted intruders—I recommend that you get in touch with an exterminator experienced in treating museum col-lections. Avoid those who apply a liquid directly on the object treated. And do not simply pick an exterminator out of the telephone book— check with local or regional museum staff people, to see whether they can recommend a suitable exterminator. One individual whom I can recommend as being familiar with specific problems in museum environ-ments is entomologist Thomas A. Parker, Ph.D., whose address is Pest Control Services, Inc., 14 East Stratford Avenue, Lansdowne, Pennsylvania 19050, (215) 284-6249.

❧ 11 ❧
Health Hazards
and
Safety Practices

S OME people may consider me an alarmist for including a chapter on safety in this book, but documented facts are available: many commonly used materials, even those in everyday service as housekeeping aids, are potential health hazards; and many commercial and workshop preparations used in conservation work are hazardous if they are not used properly.

Highly recommended reading on this subject are Michael McCann's *Health Hazards Manual for Artists* (New York: Foundation for the Community of Artists, 1978) and *Artist Beware*, (New York, Watson-Guptil, 1979). The bibliography also lists other publications recommended for anyone who works, either routinely or infrequently, with conservation-related materials. One periodical, the *Art Hazards News*, is a monthly newsletter providing current information on the subject; it and similar periodicals should be purchased by all institutions where commercial products are used in conservation work. The national fire protection association also distributes numerous publications and provides seminars on pertinent subjects. Call (800) 344-3555 for information.

Toxic Substances: Hazards that Should Be Avoided

Children's vulnerability. Before saying anything further, I should like to stress this: *children should never be exposed to the kinds of materials discussed in this chapter.* Children have little resistance to toxic substances, and there are documented cases of their developing terminal illnesses when they live in a household containing artists' studios or furniture refinishing workshops. The records also include instances of fetal damage when expectant mothers are exposed to the hazardous vapors of solvents, toxic pigments, and heavy metal fumes.

Adult need for safety practices. As for adults—who should know better—countless times people can be seen operating paint sprayers or insecticide dispensers without safety equipment and without having put on protective clothing. The situation is always the same—the spray operator squints and makes a face, frequently attempting to use one hand or the other to protect his eyes and avoid the odor of the fluid he is dispensing. The effect of these contortions is negligible: they may reduce—very slightly—the amount of spray entering partially closed eyes, but droplets of the substance being disseminated continue to land on exposed skin and eyelids. Breathing is essential for all of us, and that means that, if you do not wear an approved respirator when you dispense toxic substances with a sprayer, you will be—willy-nilly—inhaling vapors from the spray. Holding the breath for as long as possible won't help a particle; eventually, one must gasp for a lungful of air, and that means sucking in even more of the noxious vapor.

Protective clothing and equipment and approved procedures for using them are essential to the well-being of anyone working with many of the substances routinely used in conservation work. It is the responsibility of each individual who does such work—or who supervises others who do it—to see that correct safety measures are thoroughly well known and observed on the job. Institutions, their administrators and employees can now be found liable for hazardous conditions. Suggested reading is *Safe Pest Control Procedures for Museum Collections*, by Perri Peltz and Mononna Rossol, 1983. Request a copy from the Center for Safety in the Arts.

Following are some basic recommendations for doing various kinds of conservation work safely.

Clothing and Personal Equipment

Respirators. Before beginning to dispense any toxic substance with a sprayer, one should put on a well-made, properly fitting respirator, to reduce the amount of spray vapor inhaled. To be fully effective, *a good respirator must fit snugly*—bearded people cannot make a respirator fit well enough for it to be fully effective. All respirators must have the appropriate operative cartridge attached. (Here, refer to McCann's *Health Hazards for Artists.*)

Gloves. The spray-wielder should also wear protective gloves, which are available in rubber, plastic, and other materials. Safety gloves should be worn as standard equipment in working with or around noxious substances. Available are gloves of various materials—see list of suppliers. If you are like me, you will, initially, find respirators and gloves nuisances; after using them a few times, however, I found that wearing them became second nature, especially when I reflect that *I'm* the one one I'm protecting.

As a matter of course, any time you are dealing with ingredients that the skin may absorb, you need to put on a pair of disposable gloves. Maintenance people should wear protective gloves whenever they polish furniture—not to protect the furniture, but to protect themselves. Since they may polish furniture quite frequently, they should not take chances with the harmful cumulative effects that some of the preparations used for that work may have on human health.

Shop Precautions and Equipment

The emergency telephone numbers of poison centers, fire departments, and ambulance services should be posted by all telephones in the laboratory and the workshop.

Eyewash stations should be immediately available throughout the work area, in case of accidents involving toxic fluids. These stations are available at small cost from chemical supply houses, and they could save your eyes.

An "oily-waste" can, also available from chemical and safety supply houses, should be standard equipment—and should be *used* for disposing of solvent-saturated rags and cotton-tipped applicators. Use a disposable plastic bag inside the can and empty the contents of such a can, every night, into a metal trash receptacle kept outside the building. Don't allow dirty, oily rags to accumulate in the building because of the ever-present danger of spontaneous combustion. Arrange to have a rubbish company pick up your oily waste from the metal receptacle at least once a week. Do not try to burn trash of this kind: that could cause an explosion in your incinerator.

Fig. 11.1. A fume hood such as this one is necessary to exhaust toxic fumes.

Explosion-proof fans that exhaust air help carry away from the operator the vapors of questionable or hazardous materials. Such fans are available in various forms, for use with spray booths, fume hoods, fume-exhaust trunks, and as either portable or window-mounted units. Any well-equipped laboratory or workshop should have at least one fan of each of the types listed. Smaller shops and repair businesses operated from one's home should have at least either a portable explosion-proof fan or a window-mounted one. *It is important that all fans used in conservation laboratories or workshops be explosion-proof*, because flammable vapors pass through them, and a spark could cause

Fig. 11.2. Cans are safer than bottles for storing flammables.

a conflagration. Have any exhaust equipment reviewed by an engineer who's expertise is within that area. Improperly installed or incorrect equipment can actually increase the problem it is trying to solve.

Storage and Disposal of Solvents and Acids

To store solvents and flammable materials safely, always read the manufacturers' labels—and always keep those labels, if the substance is transferred from its original container. The best procedure is to store all such products in the manufacturers' container; if they *must* be transferred, however, they should be put into approved safety cans developed especially for solvent storage and labeled. See Appendix 6 for suppliers.

Waste solvents should also be stored in approved safety storage cans—which should be emptied by a licensed chemical disposal company that complies with local regulations.

It is not difficult to find a local hazardous-waste disposal company. An office of the Environmental Protection Agency should be able to provide that information. If the waste materials from a small shop or a home workshop amount only to a jar or two a month, perhaps some friend who works

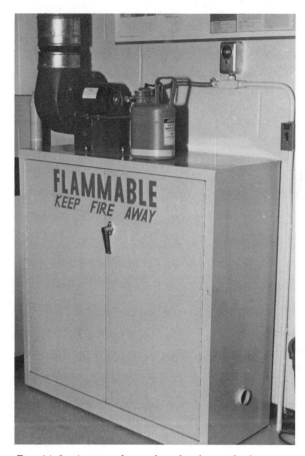

Fig. 11.3. A strongly made, clearly marked storage cabinet should be used to store the flammable materials common in any workshop or laboratory.

for a large company that disposes of toxic wastes might be willing to add those few ounces to his regular load, as a favor.

Never store acids and bases together. And when those substances are to be diluted, always pour them into water—never pour water into acids or bases.

Always wear gloves, goggles, and a safety apron when handling acids and bases.

Never pour organic solvents and acids down a drain.

Never dispose of such materials by pouring them on the ground. If that practice is followed even a few times, it could become a habit, and not a good one; you may be unintentionally creating a monster by dumping non-biodegradable materials, such as a resinous compound, a wood preservative, or something containing a pigment or particulate compound, or other potential time-bomb. Years later, after you have moved away, some unsuspecting person could plant a family garden over your dump and be poisoned by eating produce grown there.

Powdered Chemicals

When mixing powdered materials, such as dry pigments, wear a dust respirator and safety gloves. Turn on your explosion-proof fan to carry away the airborne particles. For additional information on powdered chemicals, lead hazards, fiberglass particles, noise levels, gases, and other hazards, see the publications listed in the bibliography.

Using Wood-Working Equipment Safely

When using wood-working equipment, observe the following safe practices:

1. Do not wear ties or loose clothing.

2. Turn machine circuit-breakers off when changing blades, cutters, bits, and belts.

3. Make sure you know how to operate equipment safely, under full control. One individual I know who had a part of one finger cut off in an accident with a table saw, said, later, "My mind went in one direction, then my finger went in the other direction."

4. Keep the work area clean. Sawdust on the floor increases the chances of slipping.

5. Wear safety glasses or face shields when operating machinery.

6. For protection against inhaling sawdust—the sawdust of some woods can be toxic—use particulate-matter filters in your respirator. In addition, each machine should be equipped with a sawdust-exhaust system, as specified by the manufacturer.

7. Exhaust fumes from the work area as necessary.

8. Position machines so that operators cannot be startled by anyone approaching them from behind.

9. Do not bring into the shop any food or drink that could become contaminated.

10. Never work when tired, when medication affects your thinking or co-ordination, or when you are in a hurry.

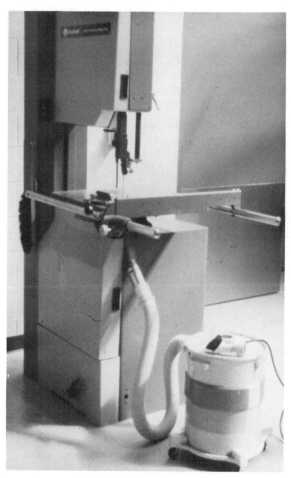

Fig. 11.4. A portable vacuum cleaner can be attached to machines to reduce dust exposure to the operator.

Substances in Common Use

A brief listing of components found in conservation related products follows. There are hundreds of other products one may encounter but this list provides a good cross section. Protection from these materials may be provided by some of the previously discussed equipment.

Material and Where It Can be Found	Affected by Exposure	Exposure Symptoms
I Methyl alcohol [1] (also labeled wood alcohol or methanol) Found in denatured alcohol, shellacs, varnishes, paint removers, paints	Central nervous system, skin, eyes	Drowsiness, blurred vision, inebriation
II Toluene (also labeled Toluol) Found in lacquers, dry cleaning solutions, paints, varnishes	Central nervous system, blood, skin, liver, kidneys	Narcosis, Leukemia Dermatitis
III Xylene [2] (also labeled Xylol) Found in insecticides, lacquers, paint removers, cleaning solutions	Skin, liver, central nervous system, upper respiratory tract	Nausea, stomach pain, narcosis, pulmonary edema, liver and kidney damage, inebriation
IV Kerosene [3]	Central nervous system, skin, upper respiratory tract	Narcosis, chemical pneumonia, broncho pneumonia, lung hemorrhage
V Turpentine [4] (also labeled Oil of Turpentine or Spirits of Turpentine)	Central nervous system, skin, eyes, upper respiratory tract	Pulmonary edema, kidney and/or bladder malfunctions, narcosis, convulsions, dermatitis

The use and disposal of hazardous materials now fall under strict guidelines issued by the environmental protection agency (EPA) and the U.S. Department of Labor Occupational Safety and Health Administration (OSHA). To aid you or your organization with compliance (stiff fines and/or jail sentences can be levied for non compliance), it is suggested that a local branch of the EPA and OSHA be contacted.

Many suppliers of health and safety supplies now offer publications and training programs. There is even a small quantity producer starter kit available from the Lab Safety Supply Company (*see* List of Suppliers, p. 213).

≪ 12 ≫
Proper Furniture Conservation:
Finding a Laboratory and a Conservator

THERE are very few well-equipped furniture conservation laboratories in the United States. This chapter says something about a lab that I know best — the Conservation and Collections Care Center of the New York State Bureau of Historic Sites at Peebles Island, in upstate New York, though this modern furniture laboratory is the exception rather than the rule. It is true that some large-scale furniture collections have major laboratories as part of their operation, but other extensive collections are not so fortunate as to have professional care so close at hand. Other types of institutions have developed conservation laboratories to care for collections of paintings and art works on paper. The equipment and supplies provided for furniture conservation, however, are too commonly only a small box of broken veneer samples, a handful of clamps—usually the wrong kind for the immediate need, a bent saw ("used last year for cutting down a tree out back"), and an empty bottle that once contained white glue.

A few years ago, two conservators whose primary work is with paintings and art on paper have said to me, "Since you are going to specialize in three-dimensional objects, you only need to purchase a few clamps, and you are in business." They were joking, of course; but it remains lamentably true that many furniture collections are in bad condition and are sorely in need of the services of a good nearby furniture conservation laboratory. Perhaps we may hope that the recent increase in the value of furniture, as evident in auction sales, will result in the establishment of new furniture conservation laboratories and the improvement of such facilities as are already functioning.

The state of New York, in the early 1970s, made a serious commit-

Fig. 12.1. The first six photographs in this chapter were made at the Conservation and Collections Care Center of the New York State Bureau of Historic Sites at Peebles Island, New York. Fig. 12.1 shows part of a work area inside the Furniture Conservation Laboratory.

Fig. 12.2. Peebles Island: dust-collecting hoses are attached to many machines.

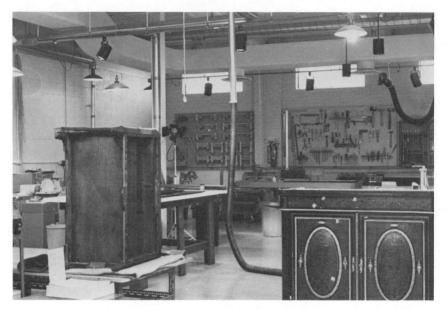

Fig. 12.3. In the foreground here is a Peebles Island laboratory cart constructed from metal-slotted angle (see fig. 9.19).

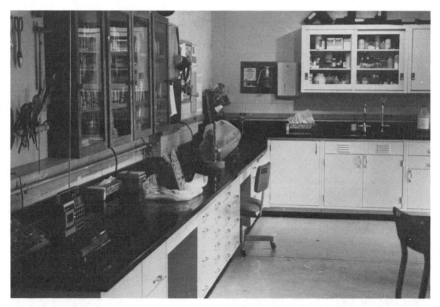

Fig. 12.4. Counter space at Peebles Island lab for microscopy and other analytical work.

Fig. 12.5. Well-made sawhorses, such as those under the piano being treated here at Peebles Island, are necessary for any well-equipped lab or workshop.

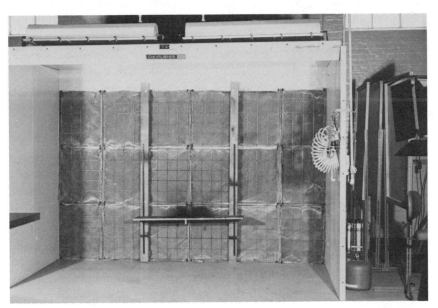

Fig. 12.6. A spray booth such as this one at Peebles Island is needed when applying finishes or working on large surfaces with toxic materials.

ment to care for historical collections in its historic sites system—collections that include paintings, paper, textiles, archaeological objects, decorative arts, and furniture.

Funds and space were provided for the furniture laboratory, and Conservation Technician Ronald DuCharme and I established it. After the initial investment had been made and we were able to move into the new quarters, we found that additional equipment was needed. We either had to buy it or fabricate it, using existing equipment. DuCharme frequently continues to design and construct special clamps, presses, and jigs needed as the work progresses. Major improvements are still being made in the Peebles Island Conservation and Collections Care Center lab, such as the gradual refining of the vapor exhaust system and the installation of humidity controls.

Adjoining the main furniture laboratory at Peebles Island are a finishing studio and a photography studio. One important item in the finishing studio is a large spray booth. Down the hall from it is a lead-lined radiography room and a microscopy room.

Services and equipment of the Peebles Island furniture conservation laboratory include—but are not limited to—the activities that follow.[1] (They are, however, limited to work needed for collections owned by the State of New York.)

1. Documenting the condition of portable three-dimensional objects primarily fashioned of wood, chiefly furniture, through making surveys of collections; conducting extensive examinations of individual objects; preparing treatment proposals; maintaining daily records of materials and techniques used during treatments; preparing treatment summaries; conducting analyses of woods and other materials; and doing specialized work in photography and radiography.

2. Conducting treatments to stabilize insecure, portable wooden objects on site.

3. Conducting treatment of portable three-dimensional objects, including furniture, on a priority basis at Peebles Island, including reproduction and replacement of missing elements; repairing inlay and veneer work; doing finish work, including staining and surface coating; stabilizing secondary and primary furniture elements; making simple upholstery repairs; cleaning objects; inpainting, scratch removal, and waxing.

4. Making available specialized advice for properly packing and transporting wooden objects.

5. Maintaining numerous machines and hand tools needed for the conservation of three-dimensional wooden objects.

6. Maintaining a wood-sample collection for wood identification.

7. Maintaining a current file of names and addresses of suppliers of conservation materials and hardware.

8. Extending advice for exhibitions showing three-dimensional wooden objects.

9. Making recommendations for the care and storage of three-dimensional wooden objects.

It is unrealistic to expect private furniture conservators to maintain a laboratory so extensive and so capable of providing such a range of services as does Peebles Island. Most conservators cannot make such a large financial commitment. Most conservators have available a good selection of tools and equipment, however, and most of them should be willing to provide many of the above-mentioned professional services, on request.

Finding a Furniture Conservator

Before 1978, it was considered unethical for conservators to advertise.[2] Since then, however, some conservators have begun advertising, so that—for the first time—the general public is becoming aware of the availability and the work of furniture conservators.

For those institutions fortunate enough to have enough money to hire a conservator, Jose Orraca's article "Shopping for a Conservator," which appeared in *Museum News* is worth reading.[3] The American Institute for Conservation of Historic and Artistic Works can also be contacted to obtain *Guidelines for Selecting a Conservator.*

One way to find a conservator is to call the major museum in a nearby metropolitan area, check with a conservation training school, or get in touch with a regional conservation center. Although these institutions may not have a furniture conservator on the staff, they should be able to direct you to one. Occasionally, conservators may be found listed in the telephone directory, although frequently such listings carry the names of restorers, rather than conservators.

At the time of this writing, furniture conservation is not a licensed profession. Membership in one of the professional conservators' organizations does not indicate proficiency. Interested persons who are not conservators can become members of such professional organizations by paying the required dues. It is to be hoped that, in future, one may enter the profession of conservator through having acquired the necessary training, experience, *and license*. Even now, however, there are certain standards that ethical conservators follow, as stated in the *Code of Ethics and Standards of Practice* adopted in 1967 by the members of the International Institute for Conservation of Historic and Artistic Works (IIC), American Group.

Generally, any reputable conservator can provide a client with a report and photographs on each individual object, describing its condition and presenting a proposal for any needed treatment, including information about materials to be used.

A cost estimate can also be furnished, sometimes given in a range of amounts to allow for unexpected difficulties. Due to the complex nature of furniture, treatment may be more complicated than was originally anticipated, and unforeseen problems do frequently arise. For example, unstable secondary elements may be uncovered, such as the problem of tacking edges of a chair too riddled with holes to accept new upholstery tacks. When such difficulties are encountered, the cost may be close to the high figure of the cost range.

In making an estimate, I usually provide a cost range. As the treatment proceeds, I keep a running account of each operation, the materials used, and the time expended. The client is billed accordingly. Usually, the bill falls below or within the range. If the treatment takes longer than my estimate, I suffer the loss, unless an agreement has been made that the client will pay additional costs.

Professional conservators also charge for survey examinations, reports, and photographs. While these items are not inexpensive, their value as documentation is worth the cost. Many times a sound conservator's report is evidence enough to persuade donors, governmental officials, and museum directors to assume their collection-care responsibilities.[4] Well-written reports have resulted in the installation of environmental controls, proper storage facilities, and the establishment of conservation laboratories.

These days, many institutions have the common problems associated with lack of funding. In the best situations, some funds may be appropriated by local friends' groups for the care of collections. Additionally, it should be possible for an administrator to budget enough to pay for a competent visiting conservator's survey and review of storage and care problems. Such reports are often helpful in persuading boards and/or governments to help in financing basic conservation methods. That approach would seem to me better than simply ignoring the problem or allowing less expensive or less capable practitioners to repair a collection.

The *Code of Ethics and Standards of Practice* of the AIC is reprinted in Appendix 1. It outlines the obligations of both the conservator and the object's owner or custodian to one another and to historic and artistic works. Copies of the code may be obtained by writing to the American Institute for Conservation.

In Part I, Section II, paragraph E, *Principle of Reversibility*, is one of the most important parts of the document. It reads:

The conservator is guided by and endeavors to apply the "Principle of Reversibility" in his treatments. He should avoid the use of materials which may become so intractable that their future removal could endanger the physical safety of the object. He also should avoid the use of techniques, the results of which cannot be undone if that should become desirable.

I should like to make this comment on Paragraph E: while it is true that *reversibility* should be held paramount—as I hope is very obvious in this book—some of the time there are exceptions, and that is covered by the word *should*.

As a specific example, if a large marble top weighing more than a hundred pounds is cracked, it is safer to avoid reversibility and reattach the pieces using the strongest adhesive available. If a weak adhesive were used, someone not aware of the mended fracture might lift or carry the marble in such a way as to cause the repair to fail, resulting in damage to the person and the marble itself—and to any other nearby artifacts, for that matter.

Many conservators will stand behind their work; this is also discussed in the *Code of Ethics*, under Section III, paragraph I, *Warranty or Guarantee*. The custodian must also be realistic. If the conservator successfully completes the treatment, and the object is returned to an unstable environment, the conservator cannot be held accountable. An example would be that of a treated piece with inlay that began to lift because of the object's being placed over a heater duct.

Usually, conservators will return to do remedial treatments for a

Fig. 12.7. Damaged furniture is examined by a conservator.

minimum fee, should that be necessary, provided that the object is cared for reasonably well.

I know of one private conservator who worked on a complex piece of furniture, encountering countless problems, for six months, straight, seven days a week. The piece was returned to its institution; and, some fourteen years later, problems again began to develop. Although not obligated in any way to do so, the conservator took the object back, spent several weeks correcting the later problems, and returned the piece to the institution at no charge.

Although that is an isolated case, it does point out that that particular conservator did what was best for the sake of the object and the client; it has been my observation that that sort of meticulous care is characteristic of the best in the field.

Note: Since the printing of the first edition of this book, the author has been personally involved with the establishment of similarly equipped laboratories in two new museums.

Fig. 12.8. The finish on this large desk has been damaged by exposure to direct sunlight.

Fig. 12.9. A mount was removed near the center of the desk pictured here during treatment. Note how the finish beneath the mount was protected from light.

Fig. 12.10. The leather top of the desk shown in fig. 12.9 had abrasions, tears, and cleavage before treatment by a professional private conservator.

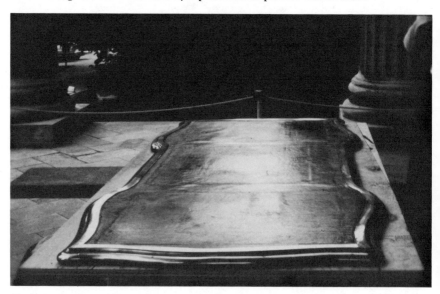

Fig. 12.11. Here, after proper treatment, the original leather top of the desk shown in figs. 12.9 and 12.10 is now stabilized. The desk top was removed for shipment.

Fig. 12.12. Treatment completed, the finished desk of fig. 12.9 is returned to its customary site. Ultraviolet-shield Plexiglas now covers the nearby window, and shutters are open only when necessary.

Code of Ethics and Standards of Practice, American Institute for Conservation of Historic and Artistic Works
Formulated May 27, 1967
Revised May 31, 1979

Introduction

The first formulation of a code of ethics for art conservators, adopted by the members of IIC-American Group (now AIC) at the annual meeting in Ottawa, Canada, on May 27, 1967, was produced by the Committee on Professional Relations: Sheldon Keck, Chairman, Richard D. Buck, Dudley T. Easby, Rutherford J. Gettens, Caroline Keck, Peter Michaels and Louis Pomerantz.

The first formulation of standards of practice and professional relationships by any group of art conservators was produced by the IIC-American Group (now AIC) Committee on Professional Standards and Procedures under the direction of Murray Pease, Conservator, Metropolitan Museum of Art. Other members of the committee were Henri G. Courtais, Dudley T. Easby, Rutherford J. Gettens, and Sheldon Keck. The report was adopted by the IIC-AG at the annual meeting of the group in New York on June 8, 1963. It was published in *Studies in Conservation*, Vol. 9, No. 3, August 1964, pp. 116–121. The primary purpose of this document was to provide accepted criteria against which a specific procedure or operation can be measured when a question as to its adequacy has been raised.

The responsibility of revising and updating the original code of ethics and standards of practice and professional relationships was assigned to the AIC Committee on Ethics and Standards: Elisabeth C. G. Packard, Chairman, Barbara H. Beardsley, Perry C. Huston, Kate C. Lefferts, Robert M. Organ, and Clements L. Robertson.

The original format has been retained except that the more general *Code of Ethics* has been placed first as Part One, followed by *Standards of Practice* as Part Two.

The revised versions were adopted by the Fellows of AIC at the annual meeting in Toronto, Canada, on May 31, 1979.

Elisabeth C. G. Packard, Chairman
Ethics and Standards Committee, 1977–79

A•I•C

THE AMERICAN INSTITUTE FOR CONSERVATION OF HISTORIC AND ARTISTIC WORKS

PART ONE—CODE OF ETHICS

I. PREAMBLE

Conservation of historic and artistic works is a pursuit requiring extensive training and special aptitudes. It places in the hands of the conservator* cultural holdings which are of great value and historical significance. To be worthy of this special trust requires a high sense of moral responsibility. Whether in private practice or on the staff of an institution or regional center the conservator has obligations not only to the historic and artistic works with which he** is entrusted, but also to their owners or custodians, to his colleagues and trainees, to his profession, to the public and to posterity. The following code expresses principles and practices which will guide the conservator in the ethical practice of his profession.

*Hereafter in the text the word "conservator" also denotes "conservation scientist" when applicable.

**In this text "he" and related pronouns are used in the classical sense to denote the person, male or female.

II. OBLIGATIONS TO HISTORIC AND ARTISTIC WORKS

A. Respect for Integrity of Object
All professional actions of the conservator are governed by unswerving respect for the aesthetic, historic, and physical integrity of the object.

B. Competence and Facilities
It is the conservator's responsibility to undertake the investigation or treatment of an historic or artistic work only within the limits of his professional competence and facilities.

C. Single Standard
With every historic or artistic work he undertakes to conserve, regardless of his opinion of its value or quality, the conservator should adhere to the highest and most exacting standard of treatment. Although circumstances may limit the extent of treatment, the quality of the treatment should never

be governed by the quality or value of the object. While special techniques may be required during treatment of large groups of objects, such as archival and natural history material, these procedures should be consistent with the conservator's respect for the integrity of the objects.

D. Suitability of Treatment
The conservator should not perform or recommend any treatment which is not appropriate to the preservation or best interests of the historic or artistic work. The necessity and quality of the treatment should be more important to the professional than his remuneration.

E. Principle of Reversibility
The conservator is guided by and endeavors to apply the "principle of reversibility" in his treatments. He should avoid the use of materials which may become so intractable that their furture removal could endanger the physical safety of the object. He also should avoid the use of techniques, the results of which cannot be undone if that should become desirable.

F. Limitations on Aesthetic Reintegration
In compensating for damage or loss, a conservator may supply little or much restoration, according to a firm previous understanding with the owner or custodian and the artist, if living. It is equally clear that he cannot ethically carry compensation to a point of modifying the known character of the original.

G. Continued Self-Education
It is the responsibility of every conservator to remain abreast of current knowledge in his field and to continue to develop his skills so that he may give the best treatment circumstances permit.

H. Auxiliary Personnel
The conservator has an obligation to protect and preserve the historic and artistic works under his care at all times by supervising and regulating the work of all auxiliary personnel trainees and volunteers under his professional direction. A conservator should not contract or engage himself to clients as a supervisor of insufficiently trained auxiliary personnel unless he can arrange to be present to direct the work.

III. RESPONSIBILITIES TO THE OWNER OR CUSTODIAN

A. Contracts
Contract practice may permit a conservator to enter into an agreement with individuals, institutions, corporations, or governmental agencies to provide conservation services, provided that the contract or agreement does not contravene the principles of ethics as laid down or implied in this code.

B. Changes in Treatment or Fee
Any changes on the part of the conservator in the contracted planned
procedure in treating historic and artistic works, or changes in the fee which
has previously been estimated should, unless circumstances intervene, be
made known to the owner or custodian and be approved in writing before
the changes are effected.

C. Abrogation of Contract
The conservator should understand that an owner or custodian is free to
select, without persuasion or admonition, the services of any conservator of
his choice or of more than one conservator simultaneously, and is also at
liberty to change from one conservator to another at his own discretion.
However, after a contract, oral or written, has been made for the treatment
of a specific object, neither the conservator nor the owner may ethically
withdraw from it except by mutual agreement.

D. Proper Course of Treatment
Inasmuch as an owner is rarely competent to judge the conservation requirements of his historic and artistic possessions, the conservator should
honestly and sincerely advise what he considers the proper course of
treatment.

E. Report of Examination
Before performing any treatment on an object, the conservator should first
make an adequate examination and record of condition. The conservator
is obliged to report his findings and recommendations to the owner or
custodian or their delegate and await instructions before proceeding.

F. Record of Treatment
A record of treatment* should also be made by the conservator. He has the
obligation to record and report in detail to the owner or custodian the
materials and methods of procedure employed in treating the object.

G. Punctuality and Expedition
It is the obligation of the conservator to estimate the length of time it will
take to complete the treatment and to abide by his contract with reasonable
punctuality.

H. Fees
Fees for conservation service should be commensurate with the service
rendered, with due regard for fairness to the owner or custodian and to the
conservator and for respect for the profession.

In determining the amount of the fee, it is proper to consider (1) time and
labor required, (2) cost of materials and insurance, (3) novelty and diffi-

culty of the treatment, (4) customary charges of others for like services, (5) the problems involved in treating a work of high value, (6) character of the employment—casual or constant client.

An owner's ability to pay cannot justify a charge in excess of the value of the service.

Conservators should avoid charges which overestimate the worth of their services, as well as those which undervalue them.

Because of variations in the treatment of similar conditions, it is impossible to establish with mathematical accuracy a set fee for a particular type of service.

I.   Warranty or Guarantee
Although the conservator at all times should follow the highest standards, and to the best of his knowledge, the most acceptable procedures, to warrant or guarantee the results of a treatment is unprofessional. This is not to be construed to mean that he should not willingly and freely correct defects or unforeseen alterations which, in his opinion, have occurred prematurely following his treatment. (Standard procedures for engaging in and reporting of examination and treatment of historic and artistic works are described in part Two, Sections IV and V.)

*Standard procedures for engaging in and reporting of examination and treatment of historic and artistic works are described in Part Two, Sections IV and V.

IV. RELATIONS WITH COLLEAGUES, TRAINEES, AND THE PROFESSION

A.   Contribution to Profession
A conservator has an obligation to share his knowledge and experience with his colleagues and with serious students. He should show his appreciation and respect to those from whom he has learned and to those who have contributed in the past to the knowledge and art of the profession by presenting without thought of personal gain such advancements in his techniques of examination and treatment which may be of benefit to the profession. The originator of a novel method of treatment or a new material should make full disclosure of the composition and properties of all materials and techniques employed. The originator is expected to co-operate with other conservators and conservation scientists employing or evaluating the proposed methods or materials. None of the above is intended to infringe upon the proprietary rights of the originator.

B. Trainees and Interns
The conservator, private or institutional, has a responsibility to undertake the training and instruction of apprentices, trainees, and interns, but only within the limits of his expert knowledge and the technical facilities available. The rights and objectives of both the trainer and the apprentice should be clearly stated and mutually agreed upon in writing, and should include such items as anticipated length of apprenticeship, areas of competence to be taught, and payments.

C. References
A conservator should not recommend or provide a reference for a person applying for a position as a professional conservator unless the conservator has personal knowledge that the applicant's training, experience, and performance qualify him for the position.

D. Intermediaries
The professional services of a conservator should not be controlled or exploited by any agency, personal or corporate, which intervenes between client and practitioner; the conservator's responsibilities and qualifications are individual and personal. He should avoid all relationships which direct the performance of his duties by or in the interest of such intermediary. This does not preclude his working under the direction of another qualified conservator, whether in private practice or within an institutional system.

E. Request for Consultation
If, for any reason, before or during treatment, the owner or custodian desires another opinion on procedure through consultation with another conservator, this should not be regarded as evidence of want of confidence and should be welcomed by the conservator.

F. Consultation
No person engaged in the profession of conservation can expect to be expertly informed on all phases of examination, analysis, and treatment. In instances of doubt there should be no hesitation in seeking the advice of other professionals, or in referring the owner to a conservator more experienced in the particular special problems.

G. Misuse of Referral in Client–Conservator Relationships
Where clients have been referred for consultation or treatment, the conservator to whom they have been referred should, unless it was obviously otherwise intended, return the client to the original conservator as soon as possible. Efforts, direct or indirect, in any way to encroach upon the professional employment of another conservator are considered unprofessional.

H. Fee Splitting

The payment of a commission or fee to another conservator or any other person for the reference of a client is to be condemned as unprofessional. Division of a fee is only acceptable where it is based on a division of service or responsibility.

I. Comment on Qualifications of Another Conservator

It is unethical for a conservator to volunteer adverse judgment on the qualifications of and procedures rendered by another conservator except as such comment shall be to the mutual benefit of all concerned. In expressing an opinion about another practitioner, either voluntarily or at the request of someone outside the profession, the conservator must always conscientiously consider the iniquity of slander and must scrupulously base his statement on facts of which he has personal knowledge. If his opinion is uncertain or dependent on hearsay, it is more constructive to withhold comment and to recommend instead someone of whom he has no doubt.

V. OBLIGATIONS TO THE PUBLIC

A. Education of the Public

In his relations with the public, every conservator should accept such opportunities as may be presented to educate the public in the aims, desires, and purposes of his profession in order that a better popular understanding of conservation may be established. Such presentations should be in accordance with accepted principles of the time.

B. Safeguarding the Public Interests

In the interests of the public as well as their own profession, conservators should observe accepted standards and laws, uphold the dignity and honor of the profession and accept its self-imposed disciplines.

C. Expertises

Although the results of his examination and treatment of historic and artistic works may make it possible for him to contribute knowledge to the history of art and to the verification of the authorship or authenticity of an object, the issuing of paid expertises or authentications may involve conflict of interest and is not an appropriate or ethical activity for a conservator.

D. Appraisals

Because of his intimate contact with and knowledge of techniques of fabrication and the physical condition of historic and artistic works, a conservator is often asked to appraise for a fee the monetary value of an object.

Since this activity may involve conflicts of interest inconsistent with the profession of conservation, and since appraising requires other specialized knowledge of market values and connoisseurship, appraisal for a fee is not recommended unless the individual is a professional member of a recognized professional society of appraisers.

E. Art Dealing
Engaging in the business of selling or purchasing for personal profit or acting as a paid or commissioned agent in the sale of historic and artistic works are activities considered to be inconsistent with the professional integrity of conservators.

F. Advertising
It is an accepted principle that the foundation of effective advertising is the establishment of a well-merited reputation for professional ability and integrity. Thus it is recommended that conservators limit all forms of notices and communications which may be construed as advertising to the following:
1. Use of such sign or signs which in size, character, wording, and position reasonably may be required to indicate the entrance of the premises in which the practice is performed.
2. Use of professional cards and letterheads on stationery, bill and receipt forms, indicating only the name, academic degree, Fellowship, conservation specialty, office address and telephone number. Only fellows may use the name of AIC.
3. Use of announcements of commencement of practice, change of location, or restriction of practice.
4. Use of advertisements in newspapers, magazines, and telephone directories, provided that their form and content do not detract from the high professional standards reflected elsewhere in this Code of Ethics and do not contain comparisons of ability and cost.

G. Solicitation of Clients
1. It is recommended that solicitations be confined to discreet announcements in newspapers and magazines inviting clients. Direct mailing to individuals, museums, and institutions may be construed as an attempt to solicit clients unethically.
2. The judicious distribution of reprints and communications to colleagues is acceptable and an author may honor requests for his articles. Indiscriminate mailing without sufficient reason is construed as an

attempt to solicit clients unethically or an attempt to bring undue attention to the author.

H. Statements in the Name of AIC
Individual members of AIC should not present opinions in the name of AIC
to outside organizations or individuals.

PART TWO—STANDARDS OF PRACTICE

I. PREAMBLE

The following standards and procedures are approved by AIC as detailed
guidelines to professional practice by conservators* in the examination and
treatment of historic and artistic works. Such practice is considered to comprise
three categories:

A. Examination, treatment, and systematic maintenance of historic and artistic works, whether by private or institutional conservators.

B. Scientific analytical study of art objects for such purposes as identifying
materials, method of construction, modifications by age or other agencies,
comparison with comparable material.

C. Supplying previously developed reference data which may bear on condition, authenticity, authorship, or age of specific objects. This can be either
by formal publication or private communication.

*"Conservators" in the text also denotes "conservation scientists" when
applicable.

II. GENERAL CONSIDERATIONS OF POLICY

These are broadly applicable to all categories:

A. Professional Attitude
It must be axiomatic that all professional actions of a conservator be governed by unswerving respect for the integrity of historic and artistic works.
Such respect is manifest not only in policies of restoration, but in selection
of courses of treatment, in safeguarding against accident, protection against
loss and strict avoidance of misinterpreting technical evidence.

B. Contractual Relationships

A contract should include the need for a clear written statement of the following: the exact work to be done, the basis for charges, if any, the extent and substance of reports, including photographs as appropriate, responsibility for insurance coverage deemed adequate for operator, owner, and object, provisions for safeguarding objects, method of delivery, and any subcontracting or reassignment of work. *

C. Assumption of Responsibility

It is a conservator's responsibility to contract for investigation or treatment only to the limits of his professional competence and facilities. Should he not be trained or equipped for a full scientific study by generally accepted current technical means, any specific limitations must be stated and accepted by both parties from the beginning. Wherever further opinion seems to be required, such further opinion or opinions are a necessary part of a comprehensive report. In the same manner, a conservator will be held irresponsible if he undertakes to carry out a course of treatment for which he is inadequately trained or equipped.

D. Interpretation of Evidence

An investigator has the obligation to present all the evidence he has developed about an object commissioned to him for study, favorable or otherwise, and also to supply from his professional knowledge a clear exposition of the significance of each part of the evidence. It will be held improper for him to make outright formal declarations as to age, authenticity, and the like (which subsequently might form the basis of a claim or legal action) when each declaration exceeds the logical development of the specific evidence.

E. Limitations on Aesthetic Reintegration

In compensating for losses or damage, a conservator can be expected to carry out little or much restoration according to a firm previous understanding with the owner or custodian, and the artist, if living. However, he cannot ethically carry compensation to a point of modifying the known character of the original.

F. Outside Activities

It shall be considered inconsistent with the professional integrity of conservators in any of the three categories of procedure to engage in the following outside activities:

1. Issuing paid "expertises" or authentication.

2. Acting as paid or commissioned agent in the selling or purchasing of historic and artistic works.

3. Engaging in such selling or purchasing for personal profit.

4. Appraising for a fee the monetary value of historic and artistic works unless the conservator is a professional member of a recognized professional society of appraisers.

*It is recommended that a lawyer be consulted.

III. PROCEDURE FOR INITIATING, CONDUCTING, AND REPORTING IN SCIENTIFIC ANALYTICAL STUDIES OF HISTORIC AND ARTISTIC WORKS

Whenever it becomes necessary for owners of historic and artistic works to request institutional or commercial analytical laboratories or private consultants to engage in scientific study of objects for the purpose of developing data which may bear on condition, authenticity, authorship, or age of a specific object, the following procedure shall be followed by all parties concerned:

A. Initiating the Study

The owner of the object, or his qualified agent or a qualified officer of an institution, shall send to the examining agency a written request with statements covering the following points as required:

1. The purpose of the study, listing any specific questions to be answered.

2. Whether (a) the whole object or (b) samples from the object are to be made available for study. If samples only are to be sent to the laboratory, the exact location of the samples on the object and the name of the person who took the samples and the date taken are to be given.

3. If the whole object is to be sent to the analyst (a) the legal owner, (b) its value, (c) to what extent it is covered by insurance, (d) by what carrier it is to be sent to the laboratory and returned to the owner and (e) that the object is to be sent to the investigating laboratory at the owner's risk and expense.

4. Explicit permission to take samples from the object during examination, defining any limitations.

5. Whether the investigator (a) is merely to report facts and observations or (b) if the investigator is expected to draw conclusion from the facts.

6. Whether the laboratory findings are (a) to be kept in strict confidence or (b) whether the findings, regardless of their nature, can be used by the investigator in formal publications and in oral declarations.

7. Whether any of the evidence produced is intended for use in legal proceedings.

B. Conducting the Study

The analyst or laboratory official on receiving the object shall:

1. Supply a written receipt to the owner verifying its condition and inform the owner how the object will be stored and guarded.

2. Inform the owner what fees, if any, are to be charged for the analytical services. If there is to be no charge, state that fact explicitly. State also what other charges may be made for photography, radiography, and for other analytical services.

3. Make a photographic record of the condition of the object and of any subsequent alteration incurred in the course of the study.

4. Keep a careful and detailed written record of all observations and findings, giving dates.

C. Preparing and Submitting the Report

On completion of the investigation, the investigator shall:

1. Render to the owner a typewritten report of his findings with conclusion, if conclusions have been requested. The report shall cover methods of testing, kind and type of instruments and equipment used, and analytical procedures employed in sufficient detail so that, if the owner wishes, the tests can be repeated and checked on the same object by an independent investigator in another laboratory. If it has been necessary, with the owner's permission, to take samples from the object, give location and amount of each sample. Give location and dosage of irradiations (e.g., exposure to X-rays, gamma rays, iridium, or other forms of radiant energy).

2. List all other persons who assisted or co-operated in the scientific investigation.

3. List what published works or authorities he has consulted in the course of the study.

4. State what limitations, if any, he may wish to place on the use of the findings. That is, whether or not the findings may be used voluntarily in legal proceedings; whether or not they may be quoted in formal publications or in oral declarations.

IV. PROCEDURE FOR ENGAGING IN AND REPORTING OF EXAMINATION AND TREATMENT OF HISTORIC AND ARTISTIC WORKS BY PROFESSIONAL CONSERVATORS OF INSTITUTIONS AND REGIONAL CENTERS

A. Report of Examination

Such reports shall include in writing the following information:

1. Date of examination and name of examiner.

2. Identification of object with the one referred to in the report by means of photographs, verbal descriptions, measurements, and identification numbers.

3. Descriptions of materials, structure, and method of fabrication. Physical, chemical, and biological identification of materials composing the object. Statement of method of determination employed or reference to published standard method.

4. Record of alteration and deterioration. Locations and extent of physical defects, chemical alteration and its products, previous repairs and compensation. Statement of method of determination sufficiently detailed to permit duplication by another examiner.

5. Deductions or interpretations of observations and analyses. Comments relative to the degree of alteration.

6. Where evidence indicates forgery, tests which can supply the necessary information on materials and structure shall be employed. After thoroughly checking his results, the examiner shall recommend consultation with one or two disinterested individuals qualified by scientific or art historical training to review the evidence.

B. Proposal for Treatment
Before any treatment is undertaken, a summary or copy of the examination record shall be supplied to the responsible custodian of the object. This shall be accompanied by:

1. A statement of exactly what conditions it is proposed to correct.

2. An outline of the proposed treatment.

3. An estimate of the probable time required for the treatment.

The official custodian's written approval shall be secured before treatment is begun.

C. Report of Treatment
Such report shall include where applicable:

1. A statement of the procedures followed in the current treatment with exact descriptions of materials and methods, including:

   (a) The method by which accretion or deterioration products were removed.

   (b) Method and materials used in correcting distortion in form and shape and in reinforcing, consolidating, stabilizing, and protecting structure and surface.

(c) Kind, extent, and location of compensation employed.

2. Photographs, as follows:

(a) Condition before treatment, with date.

(b) Photograph in "actual state" without compensation.

(c) Photograph after treatment, with date.

(d) Photographs as required to supply data about structure, method of fabrication, and state of object as revealed during process of treatment. Photographs or diagrams which clarify method of reconstruction or compensation.

V. CONTRACTUAL PROCEDURES APPLYING TO EXAMINATION AND TREATMENT OF HISTORIC AND ARTISTIC WORKS BY PRIVATE PROFESSIONAL CONSERVATORS

These do not differ from those applying to institutional conservators except in the fields of contractual relations* and assumption of responsibility. Procedures in these fields shall include:

A. Written proposals stating:

1. Work to be done, estimated charges, and estimated date of completion.

2. Arrangements for insurance and its specific coverage, method of delivery, and provisions for safeguarding objects. (See VI.B.)

3. Any sub-contract or reassignment of work proposed.

B. A signed contract by the owner or his authorized agent, which may be a signed copy of the letter of proposal.

C. Agreement to give due notice to owner or custodial institution and to receive authorization before objects are removed from operating or storage building to a new location, unless such action is required for emergency safety reasons.

*It is recommended that a lawyer be consulted as to the adequacy of the contract until such time as a standard form be adopted.

VI. OPERATING SAFETY PROCEDURES FOR CONSERVATORS

A. Safety of Personnel
All practitioners must follow the latest codes of the appropriate government regulations regarding occupational safety and health.*

1. Radiation. X-ray installation and operation procedures and use of radioactive sources should conform to approved specifications. Most

state health or labor departments will supply an inspection service to determine the operating safety of radiographic installations.

2. Toxic Vapors. Adequate exhaust and ventilation must be a part of all laboratory installations where volatile toxic materials are habitually used. Appropriate vapor respirators should be available at all times.

3. Mechanical Equipment. Power tools of all kinds should be provided with adequate light, operating space, and safety guards. Their use should be restricted to properly qualified and authorized persons. Cleanliness should be rigidly enforced. Instruments producing dust, abrasive powders and the like should be equipped with positive exhaust systems and operators should be provided with appropriate respirators.

4. Corrosive Liquids. Standard laboratory requirements for quantity storage and operating containers of acids, alkalis, and other reagents as well as solvents should be rigidly followed. Only authorized personnel should have access to them. Disposal of chemicals should follow approved procedures.

B. Safety of Historic and Artistic Works in the laboratory is of paramount importance.

1. Protection Against Environmental Hazards such as unsuitable levels of relative humidity, temperature, light and atmospheric pollution (including solvent vapors) should be provided.

2. Protection Against Theft. Working and storage areas should be of adequate construction and capable of systematic locking routine. Only authorized personnel should have access.

3. Protection Against Accidental Damage

   (a) Working and storage areas should be adequate for safe handling and storage of objects. Individual storage racks for paintings and shelves for three-dimensional objects should be available. Working equipment should include sturdy, well-designed furniture such as tables, easels, horses.

   (b) Objects should be moved or handled only by experienced persons. Auxiliary personnel should not be permitted to handle objects without adequate training and supervision. They should not engage in activities for which they have inadequate professional training.

   (c) Objects should not be removed from the operating or storage building except on due notice and with authorization by the owner or custodial institution, except when required for safety reasons.

(d) Transportation and packing of objects should be by approved agencies and according to established methods.

4. Protection Against Fire. Adequate precautions should be taken to meet the requirements of the particular insurance underwriter used. Working and storage areas should be equipped with alarm, smoke detection, and extinguishing apparatus. Uses to which other parts of the building housing the studio or laboratory may be put should not be of a hazardous nature.

*Up-to-date information may be obtained regionally through the United States Government-Labor Department/Occupational Safety and Health Area Office listed in the Telephone Directory.

PART THREE—ENFORCEMENT

Upon receipt of evidence of a violation of the AIC Code of Ethics and Standards of Practice, the Board of Directors may take action deemed necessary to protect the integrity of the Institute pursuant to the violations as referred to in the Bylaws, Section 11, 12.

PART FOUR—AMENDMENTS

Amendments of changes in this Code of Ethics and Standards of Practice must be initiated by petition from at least five members who are Fellows or Professional Associates of AIC to the Board of Directors, who will direct the appropriate committee to prepare the amendments for vote. Acceptance into the Code of amendments or changes must be affirmed by at least two-thirds of all AIC Fellows and Professional Associates voting.

Amended June 1, 1990

Conservators: A Listing

The following list should not be considered specifically for recommendations. It includes conservators who are knowledgeable in furniture conservation. Some specialize in related fields, such as musical instruments, gold leafing, frames, etc. A few of the individuals listed are not able to accept private work, while some others are exclusively in private practice. All will answer written correspondence, but I should not recommend telephoning most of them, especially where no telephone number is indicated. Try to correspond with those closest to you; and, if they are unavailable, perhaps they can recommend someone who may be available.

Another method for finding a furniture conservator (or one specializing in paintings, books, paper, architecture, objects, photographs, wooden artifacts, textiles, conservation science, etc.) is to contact the Foundation of the American Institute for Conservation of Historic and Artistic Works (FAIC) at 1400 16th St., NW, Suite 340, Washington, D.C. 20036. Voice: (202) 232-6036; Fax: (202) 232-6630. The organization provides a free date base and location of the most appropriate conservation services.

William Adair
Gold Leaf Studios
443 Eye Street, NW
Washington, D.C. 20001
(202) 638-4660

Walter Angst
2602 Evans Drive
Silver Spring, MD 20902
(301) 649-5943

Deborah Bigelow
177 Grand Street
Newburgh, NY 12550
(914) 561-6011

Ronald C. Ducharme
RD #3
Ballston Lake, NY 12019

Thom Gentle
P.O. Box 101
Williamstown, MA 01267
(413) 458-3169

S.N. Hlopoff
The Frick Collection
1 East 70th Street
New York, NY 10021
(212) 288-0700

Mervin Martin
RD #4 Box 408
Coatesville, PA 19320
(215) 486-0395

Robert D. Mussey
1415 Hyde Park Avenue
Boston, MA 02136
(617) 364-4054

Virginia N. Naude
Norton Art Conservation, Inc.
752 Germantown Pike
Lafayette Hill, PA 19444
(215) 836-1170

Scott Odell
Division of Conservation
National Museum of American History
Smithsonian Institution
Washington, D.C. 20560
(202) 357-1735

R. Wayne Reynolds, Ltd.
3618 Falls Road
Baltimore, MD 21211
(301) 467-1800

Barbara Roberts
2413 Fifth Avenue West
Seattle, WA 98119
(206) 281-9090

Tom Robinson
344 Fanshawe Street
Philadelphia, PA 19111
(215) 725-6438

Richard W. Sherin
The Strong Museum
One Manhattan Square
Rochester, NY 14607
(716) 263-2700

Dr. Michael A. Taras
Rt. 2 South Craggmore Drive
Salem, SC 29676
(Dr. Taras is not a conservator, but
specializes in microscopic identification of
wood. Please send for specific information
first.)

Jonathan Thornton
Art Conservation Department
Rockwell Hall
Buffalo State College
1300 Elmwood Avenue
Buffalo, NY 14222
(716) 878-5031

Robert Walker
Museum of Fine Arts
465 Huntington Avenue
Boston, MA 02115
(617) 267-9300 ext. 343

James A. Wermuth
32 Green Street
Newport, RI 02840

Donald C. Williams
Conservation Analytical Laboratory
Smithsonian Institution
Washington, D.C. 20560
(202) 287-3725

Marc Williams
c/o American Conservation Consortium
87 Depot Road
East Kingston, NH 03827

Susan L. Wilson
Royal Ontario Museum
100 Queens Park
Toronto, Ontario
Canada M5S 2C6

Training Programs in Conservation

Art Conservation Department
Buffalo State College
230 Rockwell Hall
1300 Elmwood Avenue
Buffalo, New York 14222
(716) 878-5025

Art Conservation Programme
Queen's University
Kingston, Ontario
Canada K7L 3N6
(613) 545-2156

Center for Conservation and Technical
   Studies
Harvard University Art Museum
32 Quincy Street
Cambridge, MA
Voice: (617) 495-2392
Fax: (617) 495-9936

Conservation and Preservation Programs
Columbia University School of Library
   Science
516 Butler Library
New York, NY 10027
(212) 854-4178

The Conservation Center of the Institute of
   Fine Arts
New York University
14 East 78th Street
New York, NY 10021
(212) 772-5800

Furniture Conservation Training Program
CAL, MSC
Smithsonian Institution
Washington, D.C. 20560
(301) 238-3700

Winterthur/University of Delaware
Program in the Conservation of Artistic and
   Historic Works
303 Old College
Newark, DE 19716
(302) 451-2479

Sample Forms Used in Conservation Work

KANSAS MUSEUM OF HISTORY
CONSERVATION CENTER LABORATORIES

FURNITURE SURVEY FORM

PRIORITY COLOR: ___Red___

ACCESSION NUMBER: _KMH, 8201_

DIMENSIONS:

CLASSIFICATION: __Domestic & Decorative Art__

OBJECT NAME: ____Arm Chair, upholstered____

GENERAL STRUCTURE: _Mortise & Tenon Joinery_

HEIGHT __33½"__ (85.1 cm.)

FRONT TO BACK 22 7/8" (58.1 cm)

SIDE TO SIDE___ 27 1/8" (68.8 cm)

CONDITION PROBLEMS: *

SECONDARY STRUCTURE

Describe _Pine apron under veneer_ &
___corner blocks present___

1. ___Generally Unsound
2. _*_Loose Joints
3. _*_Insecure Attachments
4. ___Late Elements
5. ___Battens, Plates
6. ___Missing Elements
7. ___Separated Elements
8. _*_Broken Elements
9. ___Warp
10. ___Twist
11. ___Bulge
12. ___Depression. Dent
13. ___Fill
14. ___Insert
15. ___Shims
16. ___Additional Previous Treatment
17. ___Gouge
18. ___Bent, Distortion
19. ___Split
20. ___Check
21. ___Water Damage
22. ___Stain
23. ___Insect Infestation
24. ___Other

PRIMARY STRUCTURE

Describe _Solid wood except veneer_
25. _*_Inlay/Veneer Cleavage _on apron_
26. _*_Losses
27. ___Chip
28. ___Dent
29. ___Abrasion
30. ___Brittleness
31. ___Loose Joints
32. ___General Insecurity
33. ___Late Additions
34. ___Separated Elements
35. ___Broken Elements
36. ___Wrap
37. ___Twist
38. ___Split
39. ___Check
40. ___Infestation
41. ___Stain
42. ___Other

UPHOLSTERY OR SEAT WEAVING

Yes_*_ Describe _Red Damask on_
43. ___Tear _slip seat_
44. ___Shredding
45. ___Stain
46. ___General Weakness
47. ___Loss
48. ___Infestation
49. ___Understructure Problems
50. _*_Other

FINISH/SURFACE

Describe _Darkened surface coating_
Soluble in_ Ethyl Alochol_
51. ___Cleavage
52. _*_Grime
53. ___Dust
54. ___Accretions
55. ___Stain
56. ___Finger Marks
57. ___Late Surface Coating
58. ___Early Finish Removed
59. ___Sticky Surface
60. ___Discoloration
61. ___Blanching
62. _*_Bloom
63. _*_Tape &/or Labels
64. ___Crackle
65. ___Tenting
66. ___Powdering
67. ___Abrasion
68. ___Mold, Fungus
69. ___Loss
70. ___Other Disfigurement
71. ___Other

METAL HARDWARE

Describe _____
72. ___Overpolished
73. ___Polish Residue
74. ___Abraded
75. ___Corroded
76. ___Broken
77. ___Distorted
78. ___Loss
79. _*_Insecure
80. _*_Other

COMMENTS: (Key to Above Numbers)

☒ CHECK IF ADDITIONAL SHEETS (KSHSCL–7-82) NECESSARY.

EXAMINER: _Robert F. McMffin_ DATE: Sept. 1'82

SEE OVER ⟶

KANSAS MUSEUM OF HISTORY
CONSERVATION CENTER LABORATORIES

TREATMENT PROPOSAL FORM
(See Over for Object Information)

PROPOSED TREATMENT:

1. Reglue * corner block

2. Remove modern "L" bracket. Fill holes caused by screws and repair breaks * (splice in new wood if necessary)

3. Reattach veneer cleavage

4. Replace veneer loss with new veneer matching figure and finish of original.

5. Clean surface with appropriate solvent after testing

6. Test area of bloom and correct with introduction of appropriate solvent &/or application of solution of area.

7. Remove masking tape after photography and file in labeled acid-free envelope. Remove residue from surface of seat rail.

*Adhesive used will be commercial <u>Liquid</u> <u>Hide</u> <u>Glue</u>

Est. Date to Begin Treatment Sept. 25 '82   Est. Date of Completion Dec. 20 '82

By: _____
(Project Conservation Staff Member)

Approved: _Robert F. McMiffin_   Date Sept. 1 '82
(Museum Conservator)

Concurrence: _James N. Potter_   Date Sept. 3 '82
(Authorized Custodian Only)

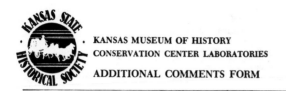

KANSAS MUSEUM OF HISTORY
CONSERVATION CENTER LABORATORIES

ADDITIONAL COMMENTS FORM   Acc. #__KMH. 8201__

Condition Problems:

   2. Front left corner block is loose.

   3. Modern "L" bracket at right leg and apron (See photograph)

   8. Breaks in above joint.

  25. Scattered cleavage adjoining loss mentioned below.

  26. 1/8" x 1 3/4" veneer loss in bottom left front of apron

  50. General overall grime.

  52. All finished surfaces covered with grime.

  62. Scattered bloom on surface of left rear leg near bottom
     (See photograph)

  63. Paper label with letters K.A.M. attached to bottom of
     left seat rail (See photograph)

Analytical Technique(s) Employed & Results:
  Microscopic identification of samples indicated.
  - white pine pimus strobus (sample from bottom of left front corner block)
  - cherry prunus sp (sample from bottom of left rear leg)

Implications of Technical Data With Respect to Probable Age, Origin and Authenticity of Object:

Symbol (e)=Estimated or Appears To Be by Examiner.
Symbol (a)=Laboratory Analysis Necessary (also applies if beyond KSHSCL capabilities or if analysis suggested at a later date)

                                Robert F Mc/Griffin
                                  (Museum Conservator)

KSHSCL-7-82

KANSAS MUSEUM OF HISTORY
CONSERVATION CENTER LABORATORIES
DAILY TREATMENT RECORD

Page _1_ of _3_
Additional Sheets

Acc. # _KMH. 8201_

OBJECT DESCRIPTION _ARM CHAIR, UPHOLSTERED_

DATE:	OPERATOR:	TREATMENT:
SEPT 25 '82	R. McGiFFiN	-PHOTOGRAPHED (OVERALL AND DETAILS) REMOVED SAMPLES FOR WOOD IDENTIFICATION. ① SQUARE BLOCK C. ⅛" REMOVED FROM BOTTOM OF LEFT REAR LEG (SEE PHOTOGRAPH OF SAMPLE AREA) SAMPLE IDENTIFIED AS - CHERRY ② RECTANGULAR BLOCK C. ⅛" X 1/16" REMOVED FROM BOTTOM RIGHT SIDE OF LEFT FRONT CORNER BLOCK (SEE PHOTOGRAPH OF SAMPLE AREA)
OCT 2 '82	" "	-REMOVED "L" BRACKET, NUMBERED AND PLACED IN STORAGE BAG. LABELED BAG PLACED IN MUSEUM STORAGE AREA FOR LATE ELEMENTS REMOVED DURING CONSERVATION TREATMENT -INJECTED GLUE (FRANKLIN LIQUID HIDE GLUE)-(A COMMERCIAL PRODUCT) INTO AREA OF BREAK IN JOINT OF RIGHT LEG/APRON - CLAMPED - SAMPLE ② ABOVE IDENTIFIED AS WHITE PINE
OCT 3 '82	" "	-REMOVED CLAMP
OCT 9 '82	" "	- INJECTED GLUE INTO VENEER CLEAVAGE (SAME GLUE AS ABOVE) AND CLAMP

CONTINUED —

KSHSCL—8-82

Private Conservators' Form (Survey)

John J. Jones

SURVEY FORM

Client _____ John L. Doe, Sr. _____ Examination Date May 10, 1981

OBJECT DESCRIPTION

Outside Measurements: Height 90" (286.0 cm)
                                            Side to Side 25" (63.5 cm)
Tall Case Clock with Works   Front to Back 10" (25.4 cm)
Owner Acc. #JDXX00188

OBJECT CONDITION

—Surface of finish is covered with grime and wax build-up
—Painted dial face has scattered areas of cleavage
—Numeral one on dial abraded in lower half with minor loss (see
  photograph)
—Left rear foot missing

PROPOSED TREATMENT

—Clean surface of finish
—Reattach cleaving paint on dial face
—Inpaint loss in numeral one
—Replace missing foot

Object May Be Accepted for Treatment after _____ May 20, 1981 _____
Estimate on When Object May Be Returned to Client ___ June 2, 1981 ___
Cost for Treatment _____ $ xxx _____

Signature _____
                        John J. Jones
                        20 Maple Street
                        Greenwood, Pa.
                        Telephone: [111] 111-1111

Private Conservators' Form (Contract)

NOTE: This form is intended as a sample only. Any contract used must conform to the specific legal requirements of the state in which you and/or the owner reside.

CONTRACT

THIS AGREEMENT dated the (20th) day of (May 1981) by and between John J. Jones, 20 Maple Street, Greenwood, Pennsylvania, (telephone number), hereinafter known as CONTRACTOR, and John L. Doe, Sr., hereinafter known as OWNER,

WITNESSETH: John L. Doe, Jr.

FIRST: CONTRACTOR will provide all labour and materials for completion of work on item(s) of OWNER, all as set forth in schedule entitled "PROPOSED TREATMENT" attached hereto and made a part thereof.

SECOND: The CONTRACTOR and OWNER understand that the proposed treatment may be modified upon notice to the OWNER.

THIRD: Upon completion of said work, OWNER will pay CONTRACTOR such amount as calculated on the basis of time and materials expended by the CONTRACTOR, to be a minimum of $XXXX.00 and a maximum of $XXXX.00.

FOURTH: The CONTRACTOR's fee shall be due and payable in full on delivery.

FIFTH: CONTRACTOR shall perform in good and workmanlike manner, and shall take reasonable precaution in the care of the item(s) of the OWNER.

SIXTH: The OWNER hereby agrees that the CONTRACTOR may use any and all photographs, drawings, and written documents made in the performance of services for scientific and educational purposes.

SEVENTH: The OWNER certifies and warrants that it is (he is, they are) the sole owner(s) of the object set forth in "PROPOSED TREATMENT" or that it has been duly authorized by the owner to instruct the CONTRACTOR to carry out the proposed treatment.

EIGHTH: OWNER represents that the maximum value of the item herein deposited with the CONTRACTOR, as described in "PROPOSED TREATMENT," has a maximum value of $XXXX.00. No claim can be made for a higher amount.

NINTH: The provisions hereof shall be binding upon the depositing institution or other owner, its heirs, legal representatives, successors and assigns.

IN WITNESS WHEREOF, THE PARTIES HERETO have set their hands and seals the day and year first above written.

_____

John J. Jones

_____

OWNER

Private Conservator's Form (Conservation Treatment Summary)

CONSERVATION TREATMENT SUMMARY

Client   : John L. Doe, Sr.
Object and Owner(s) Number   : Tall Case Clock with Works
Treatment Dates   : May 20—June 2, 1981
Photographs   : A, B & D

Treatment

—Wax build-up removed from surface
—Cleaving paint on dial face reattached
—Loss in numeral one inpainted
—Rear foot reconstructed and finished to match original

Comments

—Inpainting accomplished with dry pigments ground in resin reversible with xylene.
—New foot reattached with adhesive reversible with water.

John J. Jones, Conservator
20 Maple Street
Greenwood, Pa.
Telephone: [111] 111-1111

Private Conservators' Form (Receipt)

OUTGOING RECEIPT

Sent to:

Name John L. Doe, Sr.

Address 001 Main Street

Anywhere, USA

Description of Object(s):   RM No. 81.002

Tall Case Clock with Works

Receipt of the object(s) described above, all in good condition, is hereby acknowledged.

June 3, 1981

Date   Signature of Authorized Receiver

Partial List of Regional Conservation Centers, Associations, and Guilds

United States

American Institute for Conservation of
Wooden Artifacts Specialty Group
c/o Steven L. Pine
The Bayou Bend Collection
P.O. Box 130157
Houston, TX 77219

Arizona Paper and Photograph
Conservation Group
c/o Arizona State Archives
1700 West Washington Street
Phoenix, AZ 85007

Association for Preservation Technology
(APT)
P.O. Box 8178
Fredericksburg, VA 22404

Balboa Art Conservation Center
P.O. Box 3755
San Diego, CA 92103–0240

Bay Area Conservation Guild
c/o John Burke, president
Oakland Museum Conservation
1680 14th Street
Oakland, CA 94607

Center for Conservation and Technical
Studies
Fogg Museum, Harvard University
32 Quincy Street
Cambridge, MA 02138

Chicago Area Conservation Group
c/o Terri Sinnott, president
Motorola Museum
1261 Wiley Road, Unit L
Schaumburg, IL 60173*
*Chairpersons rotate periodically. Check
current listing with FAIC, (202) 323-
6636

Conservation and Collections Care Center
New York State Parks and Recreation
Division for Historical Preservation
Peebles Island, Waterford, NY 12188

Intermuseum Conservation Association
Allen Art Building
Oberlin, OH 44074

Los Angeles Preservation Network
c/o Christopher Coleman, preservation
officer
UCLA Library
University Research Library 11334
405 Hilgard Avenue
Los Angeles, CA 90024

Midwest Regional Conservation Guild
Conservation Services Lab
Detroit Institute of Arts
5200 Woodward Avenue
Detroit, MI 48202

National Institute for the Conservation of
  Cultural Property (NIC)
The Papermill, Suite 403
3299 K Street, NW
Washington, D.C. 20007

National Park Service
Division of Conservation
Harper's Ferry Center
Harper's Ferry, WV 25425

New England Conservation Association
Old Sturbridge Village
1 Old Sturbridge Village Road
Sturbridge, MA 01566

Pacific Regional Conservation Center
Bishop Museum
P.O. Box 19000A
Honolulu, Hawaii 96817

Panhandle-Plains Historical Museum
Texas Conservation Center
Box 967 W.T. Station
Canyon, TX 79016

Rocky Mountain Regional Conservation
  Center
2420 South University Boulevard
Denver, CO 80208

Southwest Association for Conservation
8403 Cross Park Drive #2E
Austin, TX 73754

Textile Conservation Group
c/o Vuka Roussakis, chairperson
American Museum of Natural History
Central Park West at 79th Street
New York, NY 10024-5192*
*Chairpersons rotate periodically. Check
  current listing with FAIC, (202) 323-
  6636

Upper Midwest Conservation Association
2400 Third Avenue South
Minneapolis, MN 55404

Utah Conservation Association
c/o Ellen McCrady
Abbey Publications
320 E. Center Street
Provo, UT 84601*
*Chairpersons rotate periodically. Check
  current listing with FAIC, (202) 323-
  6636

Western Association for Art Conservation
c/o Glenn Wharton, president
549 Hot Springs Road
Santa Barbara, CA 93108*
*Chairpersons rotate periodically. Check
  current listing with FAIC, (202) 323-
  6636

Washington Conservation Guild
P.O. Box 23364
Washington, D.C. 20026

Williamstown Regional Art Conservation
  Canter
Clark Art Institute
225 South Street
Williamstown, MA 02167

Other Countries

Canadian Association of Professional
  Conservators
c/o Barbara A. Ramsay-Jolicoeur
National Gallery of Canada
Conservation Department
380 Sussex Drive
Ottawa, Canada K1N 9N4*
*Chairpersons rotate periodically. Check
  current listing with FAIC, (202) 323-
  6636

IIC-CG (Canadian Group)
P.O. Box 9195 Terminal
Ottawa, Ontario
Canada K1A 3T9

Institute for the Conservation of Cultural
   Material (ICCM)
P.O. Box 1638
Canberra City
Canberra, A.C.T. 2601
Australia

International Centre for the Study of the
   Preservation and the Restoration of
   Cultural Property (ICCROM)
via San Michele 13
00153 Rome, Italy

International Council of Museums
   (ICOMUS)
Committee for Conservation
Maison de l'Unesco
1 Rue Miollis
Paris XVe, France

International Institute for Conservation of
   Historic and Artistic Works (IIC)
Perry Smith Executive Secretary
6 Buckingham Street
London WC2N 6BA, England
01-1441-839-5975

Scottish Society for Conservation and
   Restoration (SSCR)
Clare Meredith, chairman
Conservation Studio Hopetown House
South Queensferry
West Lothian
Scotland EH30 9SL*
*Chairpersons rotate periodically. Check
   current listing with FAIC, (202) 323-
   6636

APPENDIX 6

Materials and Suppliers

Two listings make up Appendix 6: materials useful in furniture conservation work and names and addresses of the suppliers from whom specific materials are available. Each list is arranged in alphabetical order, for speed and ease in use.

The materials list, which begins on this page, is keyed to the list of suppliers by number: after each product named is the number of the supplier or suppliers from whom that product can be obtained. "Abrasives," for instance—specifically, 4/0 steel wool—can be obtained from suppliers no. 32 and 67; and on the suppliers' list, suppliers no. 32 and 67 are Mohawk Finishing Products and the local hardware store.

Materials List

Abrasives
    Steel wool, 4/0: 32, 67

Acrylic Paints
    Bocour-Magna Colors: 8, 12
    Maimeri Professional Restoration Colors: 12

Adhesives
    Franklin Liquid Hide Glue: 12, 67
    Gelatin: 51
    Granular hide glue: 12, 51
    Titebond Glue and other similar yellow-emulsion adhesives [NOTE: Titebond II, a newer product, is waterproof, and so is inappropriate for use in furniture conservation.]: 12, 13, 32, 67

209

Archival supplies (see also "Storage supplies and equipment")
Acid-free paper: 12, 38, 51
Mylar: 13, 40, 51
Storage Boxes: 12, 23, 38, 51

Artist's supplies
Acrylic emulsion paint: 8, 12, 65
Brushes: 12, 65
Dry pigments: 12, 65
Gouache, watercolor: 12, 65
Plasteline (clay): 42, 43, 65
Rag-content mat board: 12, 38
Soluvar varnish: 12, 65
Turpentine: 65, 67

Chair seat weaving supplies
Cane, rush, splint, and related supplies and tools: 10

Clamps
Klemmsia and similar brands (wooden cam-action: 21, 60
Screw-type clamps with wooden jaws: 12, 14, 21, 60

Environmental monitors and controls
Humidifiers and dehumidifiers: 44
Hygrothermographs, hygrometers, psychrometers: 5, 7, 12, 18
Non-ultraviolet-emitting fluorescent tubes: 54
Silica gel and containers (to reduce humidity in small areas): 12, 15
UF-3 Plexiglas (ultraviolet filter sheets): 41
Ultraviolet shield film for windows: 64
Ultraviolet light meter: 30
Ultraviolet filter sleeves for fluorescent tubes: 48

Fillers and casting materials
Dap vinyl paste spackling compound: 67
Durham's Rock-Hard Water Putty (for casting only): 67
Low-heat burn-in sticks: 32
Magic-Stick (colored wax sticks): 32
Patchal Pencil (colored wax sticks): 32

Finishing materials
  General line of miscellaneous materials: 13, 14, 21, 32, 60, 62
  Instant touch-up marker: 32
  Lacquer (for furniture hardware and mounts): 1
  Lacquer (for wood): 32
  Shellac, dry: 32
  Shellac, liquid [NOTE: Never purchase shellac in liquid form unless container
    is dated within the last six months.]: 67
  Ultra-fine Instant Marker: 32

Gloves, disposable
  Polyethylene and other materials (see suppliers' catalogues for specific require-
    ments): 12, 18, 29

Gold and metal-leafing materials
  Gold leaf, shell gold, and related tools: 4, 12, 22, 45, 51

Hardware
  Framing supplies and equipment: 32, 50
  General line of reproduction furniture hardware from various periods: 2, 3, 6,
    13, 14, 24, 36, 39, 40, 60

Insecticides, fungicides
  Lysol disinfectant, regular grade: 66, 67
  Listerine antiseptic mouthwash (contains thymol and alcohol): 66
  Mothballs: 66, 67
  No-Pest Strips: 52, 54, 67

Insurance for art, historical artifacts, and collectibles: 25

Leather supplies
  Leather: 23, 51
  Leather dressings: 12, 51

Metal preservatives
  Manganese phospholine No. 7: 58
  Ospho: 47

Moving, handling, and shipping equipment
  General line: 9, 26, 57
  Model 512 lift (hand-operated forklift for moving heavy furniture): 55
  Movers' blankets: 26

Nails and reproduction furniture fasteners
  General line: 60
  Brass-head tacks and pins (solid brass): 2, 3

Paste waxes, ingredients, and scratch-remover polishes
  Beeswax (in cake form): 12, 51, 60
  Behlen's Blue Label Paste Wax (natural, light oak, or brown colors): 21, 32
  Butchers' Wax: 13, 60, 67
  Carnauba wax (in cake form): 12, 51
  Cosmolloid 80–11 (in pellet form): 51
  Liquid scratch-remover (for localized treatment of minor scratches): 32, 67
  Renaissance Wax: 12, 51
  Scratch-off polish (for localized treatment of minor scratches): 32
  Staples paste wax (dark brown or light): 67
  Colored wax sticks: 12, 32, 67

Photographic equipment
  Magnetic numbers and letters: 31
  Metallic paints: 31

Safety supplies and equipment
  Eyewash stations: 18, 27, 29
  Fans and exhaust systems (explosion-proof): 27, 28, 57
  First-aid cabinets: 18, 27, 29
  General line of supplies and equipment: 9, 18, 27, 29
  Oily-waste cans: 9, 18, 27, 29, 57
  Respirators for vapors or dusts (use only NIOSH-approved): 18, 27, 29
  Solvent-storage cans and cabinets: 12, 18, 27, 29

Soaps, detergents, cleansers
  Ammonia, household (non-sudsy type): 66, 67
  Orvus paste: 12, 51
  Saddle soap: 66, 67
  Soilax: 67

Solvents
  Benzine, odorless paint thinner or stoddard solvent: 12, 67

Storage suppliers and equipment (see also "Archival supplies")
    Shelving, cabinets: 9, 57
    Slotted angle (for shelf frames): 9, 15

Tools (hand tools)
    Burn-in knife, electric: 32, 60
    Carving tools, electric: 14, 19, 21 42, 43, 46, 53, 60, 62
    Framers' fitting tool (brad squeezer): 50, 51
    General line of woodworking tools, miscellaneous: 6, 14, 21, 37, 42, 43, 53, 60, 62, 63
    Jewelers' saws and saw blades: 13, 21

Wood
    Solid wood (hardwoods or softwoods): 14, 17, 28, 33, 35, 61
    Veneer: 13, 14

Workshop and laboratory supplies and equipment
    General line: 9, 18, 57
    Wood-carving benches: 21, 60
    Woodworking machines: 21, 44, 57

Miscellaneous materials
    Baking soda: 66
    Coconut charcoal (6-to-14-mesh): 18
    Cork disks (pressure-sensitive backing): 32
    Cotton: 66
    Cotton-tipped applicators: 70
    Dusting or polishing cloths: 34
    Lambs wool dusters: 49
    Mechanics' droplight: 47
    Opaline or Draft-Clean: 53
    Spray equipment: 47
    Weatherstripping: 71
    Window screen: 71

Suppliers of Materials

1. Agate Lacquer Manufacturing
   Company, Inc.
   11-13 43rd Road
   Long Island City, NY 11101

2. Americana Limited
   3902 Springhill Road
   Louisville, KY 40207

3. Antique Trunk Parts
   Martin Labude
   3706 West 169th Street
   Cleveland, OH 44101

4. Art Essentials of New York, Ltd.
   3 Cross Street
   Suffern, NY 10901-4601

5. Art Preservation Services
   253 East 78th Street
   New York, NY 10021

6. Ball and Ball
   463 West Lincoln Highway
   Exton, PA 19341

7. Bendix
   1400 Taylor Avenue
   Baltimore, MD 21204

8. Bocour Artists Colors, Inc.
   1 Bridge Street
   Garnerville, NY 10923

9. C & H Distributors, Inc.
   443 South Fifth Street
   Milwaukee, WI 53204

10. Can and Basket Supply Co.
    1283 South Cochran Avenue
    Los Angeles, CA 90019

11. Charles O'Connor Company
    P.O. Box 712
    Brockton, MA 02403

12. Conservation Materials, Ltd.
    1165 Marietta Way
    P.O. Box 2884
    Sparks, NV 89431

13. Constantine
    2050 Eastchester Road
    Bronx, NY 10461

14. Craftsman Wood Service Company
    1735 West Cortland Court
    Addison, IL 60101

15. Dampit, Inc.
    Box 493, Radio City Station
    New York, NY 10019

16. DeVilbiss Company
    Toledo, OH 43692

17. Educational Lumber Company, Inc.
    P.O. Box 5373
    Asheville, NC 28813

18. Fisher Scientific Company Head-
    quarters
    South Fadem Road
    Springfield, NJ 07081
         or
    Ottawa Administrative Center
    112 Ch. Colonnade road
    Nepean ON K2E 7L6
    (contact headquarters or adminis-
    trative center for closest dealer)

19. The Fordom Electric Company
    Bethel, CT 06801

20. Frank Mittermeier, Inc.
    3577 East Tremont Avenue
    Bronx, NY 10465

21. Garrett Wade
    161 Avenue of the Americas
    New York, NY 10013

22. Gold Leaf & Metallic Powders
    Two Barclay Street
    New York, NY 10007

23. Hollinger Corporation
    P.O. Box 6185
    Arlington, VA 22206

24. Horton Brasses
    P.O. Box 95
    Nooks Hill Road
    Cromwell, CT 06416

25. Huntington T. Block Insurance
    2101 "L" Street, NW
    Washington, D.C. 20037

26. Iden Company
    957 North Oaklawn Avenue
    Elmhurst, IL 60126

27. Industrial Safety and Security Company
    957 North Oaklawn Avenue
    Elmhurst, IL 60126

28. Kaymar Wood Products, Inc.
    4603 35th Avenue, SW
    Seattle, WA 98126
    Attention: Charlotte M. Zeller

29. Lab Safety Supply
    P.O. Box 1368
    Janesville, WI 53547-1368

30. Littlemore Scientific Engineering Co.
    Railway Lane, Littlemore
    Oxford OX4 4P2
    England

31. Magna Chart/Freed Company
    P.O. Box 4007
    Cleveland, OH 44123

32. Mohawk Finishing Products, Inc.
    Amsterdam, NY 12010

33. Native American Hardwoods, Ltd.
    Box 6484
    West Valley, NY 14171

34. Norman Thomas Company
    720 North Woodward Avenue
    Birmingham, MI 48011

35. Northwest Lumber Company
    5035 Lafayette Road
    Indianapolis, IN 46254

36. Period Furniture
    123 Charles Street
    Boston, MA 02114

37. Princeton Company Tools
    P.O. Box 276
    Princeton, MA 01541

38. Process Materials
    329 Veterans Boulevard
    Carlstadt, NJ 07072

39. Renovators' Supply
    Millers Falls, MA 01349

40. Ritter and Son Hardware
    46901 Fish Rock Road
    Gualala (Anchor Bay) CA 95445

41. Rohm and Haas
    8301 State Line
    Kansas City, MO 64145

42. Sculpture Associates
    114 East 25th Street
    New York, NY 10010

43. Sculpture House, Inc.
    38 East 30th Street
    New York, NY 10016

44. Sears, Roebuck and Company
    925 South Homan Avenue
    Chicago, IL 60607

45. Sepp Leaf Products, Inc.
    381 Park Avenue South
    New York, NY 10016

46. Simonds Cutting Tools
    2100 North Natchez
    Chicago, IL 60635

47. Skybrite Company
    3125 Perkins Avenue
    Cleveland, OH 44114

48. Solar Screen Company
    53-11 105th Street
    Corona, NY 11368

49. Spontex, Inc.
    Columbia, TN 38401

50. S & W Framing Supplies, Inc.
    120 Broadway
    Garden City Park, NY 11040

51. Talas
    Division of Technical Library Service
    104 Fifth Avenue
    New York, NY 10011

52. Texize
    Division of Morton Norwich Products, Inc.
    Greenville, SC 29602

53. Tool Works
    111 Eighth Avenue
    New York, NY 10011

54. Verilux, Inc.
    35 Mason Street
    Greenwich, CT 06830

55. Vermette Machine Company
    No. 7, 143rd Street
    Hammond, IN 46320

56. VWR Scientific
    P.O. Box 23037
    Kansas City, MO 64141

57. W.W. Grainger, Inc.
    5959 West Howard Street
    Chicago, IL 60648

58. Western Reserve Laboratories, Inc.
    1438 St. Clair Avenue
    Cleveland, OH 44119

59. William Dixon Company
    752 Washington Avenue
    Carlstadt, NJ 07072

60. Woodcraft
    313 Montvale Avenue
    Woburn, MA 01888

61. Woodshed
    1807 Elmwood Avenue
    Buffalo, NY 14207

62. Woodworker' Supply, Inc.
    5604 Alameda, NE
    Albuquerque, NM 87113

63. X-Acto, Inc.
    48 Van Dam Street
    Long Island City, NY 11101

64. 3-M Energy Control Products
    4505 Calle Mayor
    Torrance, CA 90505

65. Art supply stores

66. Groceries and drugstores

67. Hardware stores

Notes

Chapter 1

1. National Conservation Advisory Council, *Report of the Study Committee on Education and Training* (Washington, D.C.: U.S. Government Printing Office, 1979), p. 1.

2. Walter Angst, "A Case for Scientific Furniture Conservation," *Museum News* 56, no. 6 (July–August 1978): 24–28.

3. American Institute for Conservation of Historic and Artistic Works, *Code of Ethics and Standards of Practice* (1979).

Chapter 2

1. R. B. Hoadley, "Wood Has To Breathe, Doesn't It?" in *Fine Woodworking*, no. 14 (January–February 1979), pp. 80–81.

2. Robert E. Gosselin, Harold C. Hodge, Robert P. Smith, and Marion N. Gleason, *Clinical Toxicology of Commercial Products* (Baltimore: Williams and Wilkins, 1984), sec. V, p. 380.

3. Gosselin et al., *Clinical Toxicology*, sec. V, p. 374. (Listerine mouthwash states its thymol content on its label.)

Chapter 3

1. Caroline K. Keck, *A Handbook on the Care of Paintings*, 2nd ed., with corrections (Nashville: American Association for State and Local History, 1976), pp. 112–113.

2. Caroline Keck, *Care of Paintings*, p. 63.

Chapter 5

1. Angst, "Scientific Furniture Conservtion," p. 24.

2. R. B. Hoadley, "Glues and Gluing," *Fine Woodworking* 2, no. 1 (Summer 1977): 28–32.

3. I. Skeist, *Handbook of Adhesives* (New York: Robert E. Kieger Publishing Company, Inc., 1973), pp. 114–115.

4. Walter Angst, "Repair of a Side Chair with Perforated Plywood Seat," *AIC Journal* 19, no. 2 (Spring 1980): 75–88.

Chapter 7

1. Gosselin et al., *Clinical Toxicology*, sec. VI, p. 198.
2. Gosselin et al., *Clinical Toxicology*, sec. VI, p. 198.
3. R. B. Hoadley, "The Dowel Joint," *Fine Woodworking*, no. 21 (March–April 1980): pp. 68–72.
4. Gosselin et al., *Clinical Toxicology*, sec. V, p. 489.
5. Robert Mussey, "Transparent Furniture Finishes in New England, 1700–1820," Furniture and Wooden Objects Symposium, Canadian Conservation Institute, Ottawa, 1980, pp. 77–101.
6. Quoted from a lecture by Professor Rostislav Hlopoff at the Cooperstown (New York) Graduate Programs. Professor Hlopoff is now retired from the program, but still acts as a conservator.
7. George L. Stout and John R. Gettens, *Painting Materials* (New York: Dover, 1966), p. 60.
8. Stout and Gettens, *Painting Materials*, p. 31.
9. Stout and Gettens, *Painting Materials*, p. 32.
10. A. D. Newell, "Finishing Materials," *Fine Woodworking*, no. 17 (July–August 1979): pp. 72–75.
11. Newell, "Finishing Materials," pp. 72–75.
12. *Webster's New Twentieth-Century Dictionary* (New York: World Publishing Company, 1970).
13. Stout and Gettens, *Painting Materials*, p. 73.
14. Stout and Gettens, *Painting Materials*, p. 71.
15. Nancy Willson, editor, *Museum and Archival Supplies Handbook*, 2nd edition (Ontario, Canada: The Ontario Museum Association and the Toronto Area Archivists Group, 1979), p. 32.
16. Gosselin et al., *Clinical Toxicology*, sec. VI, pp. 196-197.

Chapter 9

1. Caroline Keck, *Care of Paintings*, pp. 106–107.

Chapter 10

1. Stephen Edwards, *Pest Control in Museums* (Lawrence, Kans.: Association of Systematics Collections, 1980), p. A–13.
2. Peradichlorobenzene should be used under strict guidelines and is prohibited from use in public buildings.

Chapter 11

1. Gosselin et al., *Clinical Toxicology*, sec. III, pp. 275-279.
2. Gosselin et al., *Clinical Toxicology*, sec. III, pp. 320-322.
3. Gosselin et al., *Clinical Toxicology*, sec. III, pp. 220-226.
4. Gosselin et al., *Clinical Toxicology*, sec. III, pp. 393-395.

Chapter 12

1. Robert F. McGiffin, "Care of Furniture and Other Three-Dimensional Wooden Objects within the Historic Sites System," in sec. IV of *Collections Care Guidelines for Site Managers* (Waterford, N.Y.: New York State Office of Parks and Recreation, 1980). [Not available for public distribution.]

2. American Institute for the Conservation of Historic and Artistic Works, *Code of Ethics and Standards of Practice*, revision, 1979.

3. Jose Orraca, "Shopping for a Conservator," *Museum News* 59, no. 4 (January–February 1981): 60.

4. Caroline K. Keck, "Conservation's Cloudy Future," *Museum News* 58, no. 5 (May–June 1980): 35.

Glossary

Abrasion: loss or disruption of a surface as a result of rubbing or scraping.

Accession number: specific number assigned to an individual collection object for cataloguing and/or record-keeping.

Accretion: a deposit of foreign material on a surface.

Artists' acrylic paint: paint with a synthetic medium or vehicle that carries and binds the pigment. While acrylic paints are usually supplied as an emulsion thinnable with water, they are insoluble in water on drying. "Magna" colors and Maimeri Professional Restoration Colors are also in an acrylic medium that can be thinned with petroleum solvents and are soluble in them after drying. Acrylic paints are available in tubes or jars.

Batten (also called a *cleat*): an auxiliary piece of wood attached to another wood surface. Usually fastened in an attempt to hold a panel in plane.

Benzine: a petroleum spirit or distillate commonly used as a diluent for waxes and greasy films. It has a lower flash point than common mineral spirits and evaporates faster. The term is considered archaic, with some manufacturers, because of its confusion with the highly toxic Benzene.

Blanching: the term *blanch* is from Old French, meaning "to make or become white." A whitish discoloration, in a finish, usually caused by the introduction and evaporation of a solvent or water. It can be a residual precipitate from the varnish or a leaching of some of the medium.

Bleaching: a lightening of a surface. This is a common occurrence in finish exposed to direct sunlight.

Bloom: a cloudy, whitish or bluish translucent discoloration in a finish, usually caused by the introduction of water (liquid or vapor).

Bright holes: holes in wood, caused by wood-boring insects. Light-colored holes indicate recent activity. In contrast, dark holes indicate inactivity.

Bubble-wrap (also called **bubble-pack** or **air-cap**): fused polyethylene sheets

221

with air pockets. This flexible wrapping material is used to cushion fragile objects during movement.

Check: a partial split in wood along the grain. Checks develop because of uneven tissue shrinkage in adjacent portions of the wood.

Chip: a small loss.

Cleavage: cleavage is usually a planar separation between laminae or layers of a structure, as veneer separating from the secondary wood support, or varnish separating from paint, or paint from other layers of paint, or paint from support. If separation is between laminae, that is *interlaminal cleavage;* if between laminae and support, it is just *cleavage.*

Compensate: to replace material that has been lost.

Conservation: examination, preservation, and restoration of historic and artistic works. Examination includes analysis, identification, and documentation of materials, structure, and condition. The term should not be confused with conservation of the natural environment and resources. In many countries, *restoration* and *conservation* are synonymous. That does not hold true in the United States.

Conservator: a professionally trained individual who practices the conservation of historic and artistic works. (Not to be confused with a *preservationist* or *conservationist.*)

Consolidate: to stabilize a degraded or weakened structure by introducing within it or attaching to it materials capable of holding it together.

Corrosion: conversion of metal, particularly at and near its surface, into an unstable compound due to chemical or electrochemical reactions with its environment.

Crazing: a fine network of cracking in a finish that may impart an opaque appearance to the film.

Crackle pattern: the configuration of cracks in a paint or varnish film resulting from internal or external forces acting on the film as it is drying as well as when it reaches a brittle stage. The pattern in general may be branching, as do branches in trees. Branching crackle is usually variable in width and results from shrinkage in a quick-drying film over a slow-drying one. This is often called *traction crackle.* Traction crackle resembles the surface of an alligator. Another type of crackle resembles a net. Being linear in character, very narrow and uniform in aperture, crackle is usually the result of a greater expansion coefficient in the substrate and accompanies embrittlement.

Dehumidify: to reduce the amount of water vapor in a given environment.

Dent: a concave depression caused by pressure or a blow.

Degradation: loss of original properties or stability as is seen in the discoloration, distortion, disruption, erosion, and disintegration of an object.

Disfigurement (also called disruption): a later modification that obscures or changes the original maker's intent. Disfigurement could be an accumulation of grime or stains, as well as intentional changes.

Divestment: removal of some part of the whole.

Drying oil: an oil that has the property of forming a hard film when exposed to air, in contrast to a non-drying oil, which will not form a hard layer. Through aging, the film in a drying oil becomes more difficult to remove.

Element: an individual component of the total object.

Environment: all external conditions and influences affecting the chemical and physical stability of an object. This includes all gaseous, liquid, or solid matter that envelops or surrounds the object and, in turn, takes the form of chemical, physical, and biological agents capable of interaction with the object.

Environmental controls: electrical, chemical, or physical mechanisms that can favorably regulate the environment.

Ferrous metals: metals composed mainly of iron, such as alloy steels, steel, wrought iron and cast-iron. (Non-ferrous metals, such as copper, brass, gold, etc., are generally free of iron.)

Figure (in wood): a surface pattern influenced by the wood's anatomical structure. See also *Grain.*

Fill: compensation for loss in depth.

Finish: a surface coating that can be transparent or translucent, as in the film of a freshly applied clear or orange shellac. Finish can also be opaque, as in the case of a paint or transparent film when blanching occurs.

Frass: excretions of larvae and the refuse left by wood-boring insects.

Friable: easily pulverized or crumbled.

Fungus (also called mold or mildew): disfiguring growth that often proliferates in high relative humidity, elevated temperature, and stagnant air.

Gelatin: a complex structure formed from animal tissue (usually hides and hooves). Gelatine is commonly used as a sizing material.

Gouache: opaque watercolor. In gouache, whiting is commonly added to colored pigments to increase opacity.

Grain (in wood): refers to the direction in wood of the major longitudinal fibers in relation to the plane of a finished or cut surface. Wood grain can be irregular, as it is in areas where the wood has knots.

Graining: paint and varnish layers applied to simulate wood figure. (Marbleizing employs the same materials and techniques, to simulate a marble surface.)

Grime: usually refers to surface dirt. However, grime can also be under a late finish and/or embedded in a finish.

Hide glue: a common water-soluble adhesive used in furniture construction. Hide glue is made from skin, bones, and intestines of animals.

Hygroscopic: having the ability to absorb moisture (liquid or vapor).

Inlay: a design layer set into the body of a surface for embellishment.

Inpaint: to apply paint within the boundaries of a loss of finish to complete the design. (Instain: to apply translucent stain within the same boundaries. See *Overpaint.*)

Insert: a piece of wood inserted and leveled off to the original profile of an artifact, usually to repair a break.

Joint separation: usually refers to a separation between structural elements or applied carvings and moldings of furniture. Does not apply when referring to laminated veneer or inlay. (See *Cleavage.*)

Knot: the base of a tree branch that is embedded in a tree trunk or a larger branch and is visible on the surface of wood sawn from that area.

Late: any modification of an object's original appearance that occurred after the original maker completed the object.

Loss, lacuna, void: material separated from the whole that may or may not be recovered.

Overpaint: to apply paint within, and extending beyond, the boundaries of damage on a finish.

Oxidize: to combine with oxygen. Oxidation usually contributes to degradation such as through the breaking of chemical bonds in a varnish film.

Patina: an aged appearance caused by environmental factors. Slowly developing patinas are often evidence of antiquity and should always be retained, unless the stability or the understructure of the artifact is threatened. Artificially induced patinas in most materials (including metals and finishes) are usually obvious to the experienced.

Photograph symbols:
  A = before treatment
  B = during treatment (beginning stages)

C = during treatment (advanced stages)
D = after treatment
R = raking or oblique lighting
UV = ultraviolet light source
IR = infrared light source

Polymerize: a process of joining two or more molecules of the same kind to form a more complex molecule with different physical properties.

Primary element: an element visible when the object is in its usual placement: i.e., a drawer front.

Proper side: respective to an object and not to the viewer when standing in front of the piece. An example would be that the proper right side of a chair is on *your* right when you are sitting in that chair.

PVA: polyvinyl acetate resins of various physical properties are used commonly, in solution, in conservation laboratories. PVA in the workshop also refers to polyvinyl acetate emulsions such as the commercially available "white glues."

Relative humidity: the percentage of moisture present in a given volume of air compared to the quantity of moisture that volume of air could hold at saturation (100 percent) at the same temperature.

Restoration: to return an object to its original appearance and condition. In many countries (other than the United States) restoration is synonymous with conservation.

Restorer: one who practices restoration.

Reversibility: the use of techniques and/or materials that allow a repairing process to be undone.

Secondary element: an element that is not visible when the object is in its usual placement: i.e., a drawer bottom or the back of a case piece.

Shelf-life: the length of time that a material is useful. Beyond this time, the material's physical properties change. An example would be an old shellac that will never dry properly.

Shim: a strip of material, usually wood, used to fill a space in a secondary structure. Shims are also commonly used to level an object.

Size (or sizing): a material used to seal (or prime) a porous surface.

Splice: usually refers to the joining of an insert.

Split: a continued break in a piece of wood (see *Check*).

Stabilize: to make secure, as in reattaching joint separations and/or cleavage.

Strip: to remove a finish.

Support element: a foot, leg, or any device used to hold an object upright and incorporated into the design by the original maker.

Surface film: a transparent, translucent, or opaque surface layer (see *Finish*).

Toning: changing the appearance of a furniture surface coating or of the wood itself.

Tone down: to reduce the appearance of scratches or abrasions through the introduction of a paint, stain, or other colored material.

Veneer: a thin layer, usually of wood, whose primary function is to add embellishment. Veneer is attached to a secondary understructure.

Warp: a concave or convex planar distortion parallel to the tree-stem axis. (A bend would be a distortion at right angles to the tree-stem axis.)

Wax build-up: surface accumulation of various polishes and/or waxes. A wax build-up may also be impregnated with grime and other foreign staining materials.

Wood-borer: insect (adult or larvae) that tunnels through wood contributing to the general degradation of the structure.

Wood surface:

    Radial: surface exposed by a longitudinal cut made at right angles to the growth increments and parallel to the rays.

    Tangential: surface exposed by a longitudinal cut at right angles to the rays and tangent to the growth increments.

    Transverse (also called cross-section): surface exposed by a cut made at right angles to the grain (see *Grain*).

Bibliography

The American Institute for Conservation of Historic and Artistic Works. *Code of Ethics and Standards of Practice*. Washington, D.C., 1980.

Angst, Walter. 'A Case for Scientific Furniture Conservation.' *Museum News* 56, no. 6 (July/August 1978).

Bigelow, Deborah. *Gold Leaf on Furniture: Its History, Application and Conservation*, an unpublished dissertation for the London College of Furniture. London, England, 1982. (Write to Deborah Bigelow, Furniture Conservator, 177 Grand Street, Newburgh, New York 12505, to obtain a copy.)

Florian, M., "The Freezing Process—Effects on Insects and Artifact Materials," *Leather Conservation News*, Vol. 3, Number 1, Materials Conservation Laboratory, Austin, 1986.

Gosselin, Robert E.; Hodge, Harold C.; Smith, Roger P.; and Gleason, Marion N. *Clinical Toxicology of Commerical Products*. Fifth Edition. Baltimore: The Williams Y. Wilkins Co., 1984.

Hoadley, R. B. "The Dowel Joint." *Fine Woodworking*, no. 21 (March/April 1980).

_____ . "Glues and Gluing." *Fine Woodworking* 2, no. 1 (Summer 1977).

_____ . "Wood." *Fine Woodworking* 1, no. 3 (Summer 1976).

_____ . "Wood Has To Breathe, Doesn't It?" *Fine Woodworking*, no. 14 (January/February 1979).

Keck, Caroline K. *A Handbook on the Care of Paintings*. Nashville: American Association for State and Local History, 1979.

_____ . *Safeguarding Your Collection in Travel*. Nashville: American Association for State and Local History, 1970.

Kushel, D. *Photodocumentation for Conservation: Procedural Guidelines and Photographic Concepts and Techniques*. American Institute for Conservation of Historic and Artistic Works, 1980.

Lafontaine, R. H. *Environmental Norms for Canadian Museums, Art Galleries, and Archirves*. Technical Bulletin no. 5, Ottawa, Canada: Canadian Conservation Institue, 1979.

_____ . *Recommended Environmental Monitors for Museums,Archives, and Art Galleries*. Technical Bulletin no. 7. Ottawa, Canada: Canadian Conservation Institute, 1980.

McCann, M. *Health Hazards Manual for Artists*. New York: Foundation for the Community of Artists, 1978.

McGiffin, R. F. *A Current Status Report on Fumigation in Museums and Historical Agencies*. Nashville: American Association for State and Local History, 1985.

_____. "Furniture Conservation." *Fine Woodworking*, no. 22 (May/June 1980).

_____. "Health and Safety in the Museum Workplace." *Museum News*, vol. 64, number 2 (December 1985) pp. 36-43.

Macleod, K. J. *Museum Lighting*. Technical Bulletin no. 2. Ottawa, Canada: Canadian Conservation Institute, 1978.

_____. *Relative Humidity*. Technical Bulletin no. 1. Ottawa, Canada: Canadian Conservation Institute, 1978.

Mactaggart, Peter and Ann. *Practical Guilding*. Welwyn, Herts, England: Mac and Me, Ltd., 1985.

Newell, A. D. "Finishing Materials." *Fine Woodworking*, no. 17 (July/August 1979).

The Ontario Museum Association and the Toronto Area Archivists Group. *Museum and Archival Supplies*. Ontario, Canada, 1978.

Rossol, M., *The Artist's Complete Health & Safety Guide*, North Light Books, Cincinnati, 1990.

Stolow, Nathan. *Conservation and Exhibitions, Packing, Transport, Storage and Environmental Considerations*. Boston: Butterworths, 1987.

Story, Keith O. *Approaches to Pest Management in Museums*. Suitland, Maryland: Smithsonian Institution, 1985.

Stout, George L., and Gettens, John R. *Painting Materials*. New York: Dover Publications, Inc., 1966.

Thomason, G. *The Museum Environment*. Boston: Butterworths, 1978.

Williams, Marc A. *Keeping It All Together*. Worthington, Ohio: Ohio Antique Review, Inc., 1988.

Younghans, S. & Anderson, G., *A Holistic Approach To Museum Pest Management*, American Association for State and Local History, Nashville, 1990.

Zycherman, L., Editor, *A Guide to Museum Pest Control*, The Association of Systematics Collections, Washington, D.C., 1990.

Useful Periodicals:

Art Hazard News, published by the Center for Safety in the Arts, 5 Beekman Street, Suite 1030, New York, New York 10038

Canadian Conservation Institute Publications (CCI), 1030 Innes Road, Ottawa, Ontario K1A OC8, Canada, produces periodic publications of significant interest.

Fine Woodworking, published by the Taunton Press, Inc., Newtown, Connecticut 06470.

Guidelines for Selecting a Conservator (1985), FIAC, Washington, D.C. 20007

History News and *History News Dispatch*, published by the American Association for State and Local History, 172 Second Avenue North, Nashville, Tennessee 37201.

Museum News, published by the American Association of Museums, 1055 Thomas Jefferson Street, N.W., Washington, D.C. 20007.

The Old-House Journal, 69A Seventh Avenue, Brooklyn, New York 11217.

PICTURE CREDITS

Except for two jacket photographs and photographs 9.1 and 9.2, all photographs that appear in this book were made by the author. The objects that appear in many of the photographs are reproduced here by permission of their owners, whose names follow.

Anonymous
Figs. 2.3, 4.1, 4.7 and 5.11.

Historic Cherry Hill
Albany, New York 12202: Figs. 5.26 and 7.4

National Park Service
Martin Van Buren National Historic Site
Kinderhook, New York 12106: Figs. 7.8, 7.9.

New York State Office of Parks and Recreation
Division for Historic Preservation
Bureau of Historic Sites
Private collections: 1.4, 1.5, 1.6, 1.8; 2.3; 3.1, 3.4; 5.7, 5.9, 5.19, 5.20; 6.4, 6.5, 6.7, 6.8, 6.9, 6.10, 6.15, 7.5, 7.7; 9.7; 11.2.
Rensselaer County Historical Society, Troy, New York 12182: Figs. 6.13, 6.14, 6.16, 6.17, 6.18, 6.19, 6.20, 6.21, 6.22, and 6.23.

Index